BBC
goodfood
eatwell
LOW-SUGAR
RECIPES

10 9 8 7 6 5 4 3

BBC Books, an imprint of Ebury Publishing
20 Vauxhall Bridge Road,
London SW1V 2SA

BBC Books is part of the Penguin Random House group of companies whose addresses can be found at
global.penguinrandomhouse.com

Penguin
Random House
UK

Photographs © BBC Worldwide, 2015
Recipes © BBC Worldwide, 2015
Book design © BBC Worldwide, 2015

First published by BBC Books in 2015

www.eburypublishing.co.uk

A CIP catalogue record for this book is available from the British Library

ISBN 9781849909006

Printed and bound in China by Leo Paper Products Ltd.
Colour origination by Dot Gradations Ltd, UK

Commissioning editor: Lizzy Gray
Editorial manager: Lizzy Gaisford
Project editor: Helena Caldon
Designers: Interstate Creative Partners Ltd
Design manager: Kathryn Gammon and Annette Peppis
Production: Alex Goddard

Penguin Random House is committed to a sustainable future
for our business, our readers and our planet. This book is made
from Forest Stewardship Council® certified paper.

MIX
Paper from
responsible sources
FSC® C018179

PICTURE AND RECIPE CREDITS

BBC Good Food magazine and BBC Books would like to thank the following people for providing photos. While every effort has
been made to trace and acknowledge all photographers, we should like to apologize should there be any errors or omissions.

David Grennan p133, p177; Will Heap p43, p63, p79, p101, p135, p139, p149, p173; Lara Holmes p55; Gareth Morgans p59, p77,
p85, p95, p103, p105, p109, p111, p117; David Munns p49, p51, p69, p91, p97, p107, p119, p123, p141, p181; Myles New p27, p33,
p61, p81, p93, p113, p127, p131, p185; Stuart Ovenden p65, p115, p143, p157; Lis Parsons p37, p57, p71, p87, p129; William Reavell
p75; Charlie Richards p39, p67; Howard Shooter p73; Simon Smith p145, p163, p165; Sam Stowell p25, p147, p151, p153, p155,
p159, p161, p167, p169, p171; Yuki Sugiura p53; Martins Thompson p187; Simon Walton p63, p89, p125; Philip Webb p45, p47, p121,
p137, p175; Simon Wheeler p41.

All the recipes in this book were created by the editorial team at Good Food and by regular contributors to BBC magazines.

LOW-SUGAR RECIPES

Editor **Kerry Torrens**

BOOKS

Contents
. . . .

ntroduction
· · · · · · · · · · · · · · · · · · · ·

you're looking for more energy, a
etter mood and want to feel lighter
nd healthier, this is the book for you.
he recipes in these pages have been
elected to take you through the day
ne low-sugar way and, because we all
eed a little sweetness in our lives from
ime to time, we've included some
elicious low-sugar desserts, bakes and
ven a cake or two. So whether you
vant a protein-packed breakfast to set
ou up for the day ahead or you still
vant to have your cake and eat it, we
hink you'll be amazed by the variety of
elicious low-sugar recipes on offer.

Vhat's wrong with sugar?

Over recent years the amount of sugar
ve've all been eating has increased
dramatically as more of the sweet stuff
s added to the foods we eat – not just in
zzy drinks and the more frequent
:akes, bakes and puds but also in more

surprising products, such as pasta
sauces, savoury soups and healthy
breakfast cereals.

Of course, we do need some sugar in
our diet to fuel our muscles and keep
our brain on an even keel, but we get
plenty of what our body needs, in the
form of glucose, from the starchy carbs
we eat. Foods like rice, bread and
potatoes are all fabulous sources of the
energy we require to get us through the
day – what's more, as an added bonus,
they supply the additional nutrients that
our bodies need too. Sugar, on the
other hand, supplies empty calories – it
gives us that fast kick of energy that is
quickly followed by a crash and the
associated irritability, tiredness and
need for another sugar fix.

Low-sugar diets are widely believed to
be the healthy option as more and more
evidence reveals to us how damaging

sugar is. That's because eating too much sugar leads to extra weight gain, which as a consequence increases our risk of health issues, including type-2 diabetes and heart disease as well as breast and colon cancers. But that's not all, our sugar overload is also responsible for mood swings, premature skin ageing and poor dental health.

Do not fear, though, all this doesn't mean you can't ever have sugar – that would be unrealistic – but it does mean that we should be aware of where sugar appears in our diet and try to make sure that we're not becoming over-reliant on it.

Break the cycle

Cutting down on the sweet stuff may sound tough, but it needn't leave a bitter taste, thanks to our specially selected low-sugar recipes. As always,

the results from our *Good Food* recipes are guaranteed, because all of them have been triple-tested to ensure they will work for you in your own kitchen, every time. So whether you're throwing a dinner party and want to impress or you want something sweet and light for the cake tin, the pages of this little book hold the answer.

A low-sugar diet is actually at the heart of all healthy, balanced eating plans and can be easier to stick to than you might think. First, you need to ditch the sugar bowl to help wean your palate off sweet tastes; enjoy cakes, bakes and chocolate as an occasional treat only, and wise up on the hidden sugars in the foods that you buy by scrutinising their labels.

Understanding the effect that different carbs have on your blood sugar is the key to controlling your sugar 'need'. Try

base your diet around carbs that are
gested more slowly, as this will help
eep blood-sugar levels even, sustain
our energy levels and, what's more, it'll
elp you resist the biscuit barrel. These
ecipes use slow-release carbs that
ature in a low GI (Glycaemic Index)
iet – those with fibre, such as brown
ce and wholewheat pasta and grains,
ich as rye and oats. Finally, try to
repare and cook more of your meals
nd snacks from scratch using fresh,
nprocessed ingredients; that way you'll
now exactly what has been used to
weeten them.

hat's the alternative?

idly, sugar substitutes aren't the
nswer because they won't cure your
veet tooth – it's only by cutting back
n the sweetness in your diet that you'll
etrain your palate. However, there are
ccasions when a sweet taste lifts a

recipe, and it's especially relevant when
you're cooking for a celebration or a
dinner party. You'll notice that for a
number of our 'sweet' treats, such as
the delicious *Baked banana
cheesecake* and our zesty *Moroccan
orange and cardamon cake*, we've
used the sweetness of fruit or a natural
sweetener, like xylitol.

Here are some of the options available
to you:

Stevia is a calorie-free alternative to
sugar, which is made from the leaves of
a plant that contains sweet-tasting
compounds called steviol glycosides.
Stevia is up to 400 times sweeter than
sugar, so the amount you use is tiny in
comparison to the real thing. What's
more, it doesn't impact blood-sugar
levels. It is available in supermarkets
and health-food shops as granules or
tablets, or in liquid form.

Xylitol, despite its synthetic-sounding name, is derived from the woody fibres of plants; it looks like sugar, but it contains 40 per cent fewer calories, has a low GI and actually protects teeth from decay. It has around the same sweetness as sugar and is available in powder and granule form. You can use xylitol as a substitute in many recipes (at a ratio of 1:1), but not for those that use yeast as a raising agent.

Maple syrup is an altogether smarter way to enjoy a little sweetness, and that's because as well as being deliciously sweet it's also a valuable source of minerals, including the immune-supportive mineral zinc, as well as protective compounds called polyphenols. Don't forget, maple syrup is a source of sugar and will still impact your blood-sugar levels.

Honey is another popular choice and works well in moist, dense full-flavoured bakes. It's sweeter than sugar, so you'll need to use less of it, and because honey is liquid you'll need less fluid (approximately one-fifth less). Don't be fooled, though, honey is still high in calories, and because it is rich in glucose it causes elevations in blood sugar, so use it sparingly.

Agave nectar (or syrup) can be used in place of syrups like golden syrup. It's available in mild or rich flavours, has a low GI but, being about 30 per cent sweeter than sugar, you'll need less to achieve the same taste. It works well in chewy bakes like flapjacks as well as sticky cakes or muffins. It's a liquid, which means you'll need to reduce the amount of other fluids in the recipe, and it benefits from cooking at a lower temperature (reduce the cooking

temperature by about 10C/50F). Agave nectar is high in fructose, which is thought to be one of the most damaging forms of sugar, so always use it in small quantities and buy the organic, raw agave rather than the cheaper, highly processed version.

The crafty cook's strategies to low-sugar baking

We all love to bake, so you'll be pleased to hear that there are plenty of crafty ways in which you can reduce the amount of sugar you use without resorting to sugar substitutes.

Naturally sweet ingredients like fresh, frozen or dried fruits, including apricots, bananas, dates, raisins and figs, as well as grated sweet vegetables, like carrots, parsnips and beetroot, all work well. Using these ingredients also adds moisture and density to your bake, as well as fibre and other valuable nutrients, including minerals such as potassium and iron. When using fresh produce always choose the ripest you can find to get the full benefit of its natural sweetness.

As you lower the sugar content of your favourite sweet recipes, experiment by adding flavour with cinnamon, vanilla, nutmeg and ginger, or use nuts, such as ground almonds, chopped walnuts and even coconut.

Why this little book?
This recipe book is designed to ensure that while you're following a low-sugar diet you won't feel deprived. What's more, we've done all the hard work for you, because each of our recipes has been analysed on a per-serving basis.

This means you can see exactly the amount of total sugars that a serving of each dish supplies – to qualify as 'low sugar' all of the recipes selected contain 15g total sugar or less per portion.

Remember, as with any healthy-eating plan, preparation is key, so arm yourself with the correct information and be prepared to explore new ways to enjoy a little sweetness in your diet.

If you're prone to sugar cravings, always start the day well. Swap your carb-rich breakfast cereal or toast and jam for a more sustaining start to the day, such as our *Dippy eggs with Marmite soldiers*. A filling breakfast helps to stabilise blood-sugar levels – making you less likely to need a sweet boost later in the day. A protein-packed lunch is a sure-fire way to get you through that mid-afternoon danger zone, so ditch the pasta salad or doorstep sandwich in favour of our *Spanish spinach omelette* or *Spicy chicken salad with broccoli*.

So what are you waiting for? Make this little book your new best friend, and you will find yourself enjoying a lighter, healthier way of cooking and eating.

Kerry

Kerry Torrens
Good Food magazine

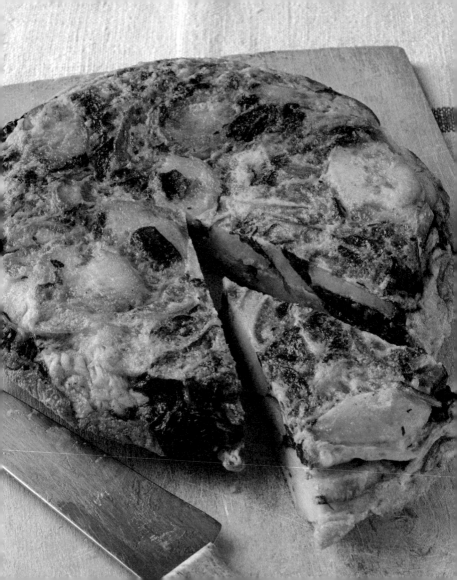

Notes &
conversion tables

NOTES ON THE RECIPES
- Eggs are large in the UK and Australia and extra large in America unless stated.
- Wash fresh produce before preparation.
- Recipes contain nutritional analyses for 'sugar', which means the total sugar content including all natural sugars in the ingredients, unless otherwise stated.

OVEN TEMPERATURES

GAS	°C	°C FAN	°F	OVEN TEMP.
¼	110	90	225	Very cool
½	120	100	250	Very cool
1	140	120	275	Cool or slow
2	150	130	300	Cool or slow
3	160	140	325	Warm
4	180	160	350	Moderate
5	190	170	375	Moderately hot
6	200	180	400	Fairly hot
7	220	200	425	Hot
8	230	210	450	Very hot
9	240	220	475	Very hot

APPROXIMATE WEIGHT CONVERSIONS
- All the recipes in this book list both metric and imperial measurement Conversions are approximate and have been rounded up or down. Follow one set of measurements only; do not mix the two.
- Cup measurements, which are use in Australia and America, have not been listed here as they vary from ingredient to ingredient. Kitchen scales should be used to measure dry/solid ingredients.

Good Food is concerned about sustainable sourcing and animal welfare. Where possible, humanely reared meats, sustainably caught fish (see fishonline.org for further information from the Marine Conservation Society) and free-rang chickens and eggs are used when recipes are originally tested.

POON MEASURES

oon measurements are level unless otherwise specified.

1 teaspoon (tsp) = 5ml

1 tablespoon (tbsp) = 15ml

1 Australian tablespoon = 20ml (cooks in Australia should measure 3 teaspoons where 1 tablespoon is specified in a recipe)

PPROXIMATE LIQUID CONVERSIONS

ETRIC	IMPERIAL	AUS	US
0ml	2fl oz	¼ cup	¼ cup
25ml	4fl oz	½ cup	½ cup
75ml	6fl oz	¾ cup	¾ cup
25ml	8fl oz	1 cup	1 cup
00ml	10fl oz/½ pint	½ pint	1¼ cups
50ml	16fl oz	2 cups	2 cups/1 pint
00ml	20fl oz/1 pint	1 pint	2½ cups
litre	35fl oz/1¾ pints	1¾ pints	1 quart

Creamy yogurt porridge

Low in fat, sugar and calories, this breakfast keeps you full all morning. Top with seasonal berries, apple or pear and sprinkle with blood-sugar-balancing cinnamon.

 4 minutes 1

- 3 tbsp porridge oats
- 150g pot 0%-fat probiotic yogurt

1 Tip 200ml/7fl oz water into a small non-stick pan and stir in the porridge oats.
2 Cook over a low heat until bubbling and thickened. (To make in a microwave, cook for 3 minutes on High in a deep container; this will prevent spillage as the mixture will rise up as it cooks.)
3 Stir in all the yogurt now or swirl in half now and top with the rest when served up. Serve plain or with one of our suggested toppings.

PER SERVING 184 kcals, protein 13g, carbs 26g, fat 2g, sat fat none, fibre 3g, sugar 13g, salt 0.4g

Almond nut butter

· ·

Blitz up your own homemade nut butter for spreading on toast, filling pancakes or adding to sauces.

🕐 10 minutes   🥧 16–18 tbsp

- 250g/9oz blanched almonds
- 2 tbsp mild oil, such as coconut, almond or olive oil

1 Put the almonds in a food processor and blitz on high until finely chopped and the nuts have come together to form a thick ball. With the processor still running, add the oil, 1 teaspoon at a time, until the mixture is a smooth, glossy paste – about 7 minutes.

2 Spoon into a clean jar and keep tightly closed and chilled when not in use. Will keep in the fridge for up to 3 weeks.

· ·
PER TBSP 99 kcals, protein 3g, carbs 1g, fat 9g, sat fat 2g, fibre 2g, sugar 1g, salt none

Dippy eggs with Marmite soldiers

Start the day the right way, with this quick, easy and nutritious breakfast.

 10 minutes   2

- 2 eggs
- 4 slices wholemeal bread
- knob butter
- Marmite, for spreading
- few mixed seeds, to coat (optional)

1 Bring a pan of water to a simmer. Add the eggs, simmer for 2 minutes if room temp, 3 minutes if fridge-cold, then turn off the heat. Cover the pan and leave for 2 minutes more.

2 Meanwhile, toast the wholemeal bread and spread thinly with butter, then Marmite. To serve, cut the toast into soldiers and dip into the egg, then a few mixed seeds, if you like.

PER SERVING 372 kcals, protein 17g, carbs 31g, fat 21g, sat fat 8g, fibre 4g, sugar 2g, salt 1.09g

Broccoli & poached-egg toasts

This may sound like an unusual way to enjoy your breakfast eggs, but broccoli is a blood-sugar wonder and by eating it you'll be contributing to your 5-a-day.

 25 minutes 4

- 225g/8oz purple sprouting broccoli
- 1 ciabatta loaf
- 1 garlic clove, halved
- 2 tbsp olive oil
- 1 tbsp Dijon mustard
- 6 shallots, halved lengthways
- 4 eggs

1 Slice the broccoli and blanch in boiling water for 1 minute. Drain and refresh in cold water. Dry on kitchen paper. Set aside. Heat a griddle or frying pan until hot.

2 Cut the ciabatta in half horizontally, then cut each slice in half. Rub with the cut garlic and brush with half the oil. Cook the ciabatta on the griddle or in the pan for 1–2 minutes each side until golden. Spread with mustard and keep warm. Toss the shallots in the remaining olive oil and cook cut-side down on the griddle or in the pan for 2 minutes each side. Keep warm.

3 Pile the broccoli on to the griddle or into the pan and cook for 3–4 minutes, turning frequently. Meanwhile, poach the eggs in gently simmering water until set to your liking. Pile the shallots and broccoli on the ciabatta. Top with the eggs and season to serve.

PER SERVING 350 kcals, protein 17g, carbs 36g, fat 14g, sat fat 3g, fibre 4g, sugar 4g, salt 1.6g

All-in-one baked mushrooms

This easy breakfast-come-dinner is a versatile recipe to have up your sleeve for when you need a protein-packed start to the day or a satisfying evening meal.

 30 minutes 2

- 2 tbsp olive oil
- 4 very large field mushrooms
- 4 slices good-quality cooked ham
- 4 eggs

1 Heat oven to 220C/200C fan/gas 7. Drizzle a little of the olive oil over the base of a ceramic baking dish then pop in the mushrooms. Drizzle with the remaining oil and season. Bake for 15 minutes until soft, then remove from the oven.

2 Tuck the ham slices around the mushrooms to create little pockets. Crack the eggs into the pockets, then return to the oven for 10 minutes until the egg white is set and the yolk is still a little runny. Serve straight from the dish.

PER SERVING 379 kcals, protein 30g, carbs 1g, fat 28g, sat fat 6g, fibre 3g, sugar 1g, salt 1.79g

Bacon & parsley hotcakes

Perfect for a lazy brunch or a quick supper – make life even easier by preparing the dry mix the night before, then stir in the eggs and milk when needed.

 25 minutes 4

- 100g/4oz smoked bacon lardons
- 100g/4oz self-raising flour
- 50g/2oz grated mature Cheddar cheese
- 1 tsp thyme leaves or ½ tsp dried, plus extra sprigs to garnish (optional)
- 2 tbsp chopped parsley leaves
- 2 eggs
- 6 tbsp milk
- sunflower oil, for frying
- poached eggs and crème fraîche, to serve

1 Dry-fry the lardons until crisp and golden. Tip on to a plate to cool. Mix the flour, cheese, herbs, lardons, some salt and black pepper in a bowl. Make a well in the centre and drop in the eggs. Beat with a wooden spoon, then gradually add the milk, drawing the flour into the centre as you go. You should end up with a fairly thick batter.

2 Heat a little oil in a frying pan, drop in large spoonfuls of the batter, then cook until the hotcakes start to set around the edges. Flip them over, then cook until golden. Keep warm while you cook the remaining hotcakes.

3 Serve each person two hotcakes topped with a poached egg and a spoonful of crème fraîche, garnishing with an extra thyme sprig, if you like.

PER SERVING 263 kcals, protein 14g, carbs 19g, fat 14g, sat fat 6g, fibre 1g, sugar 1g, salt 1.3g

Perfect pancakes

· ·

A foolproof batter recipe – serve with seasonal fruit, a dollop of natural yogurt and a sprinkle of chopped nuts.

🕐 30 minutes   🥧 8

- 100g/4oz plain flour
- pinch salt
- 2 eggs
- 300ml/½ pint semi-skimmed milk
- 1 tbsp sunflower or vegetable oil, plus extra for frying

1 Put the flour and salt into a large mixing bowl. Crack in the eggs, then pour in 50ml/2fl oz of the milk and the oil. Whisk together to incorporate the flour, then beat to a smooth, thick paste. Add more milk if necessary.

2 Pour in the remaining milk in a steady stream, whisking, until the batter is the consistency of slightly thick single cream.

3 Heat a frying pan over a moderate heat and wipe with oiled kitchen paper. Ladle some batter into the pan, tilting it to spread in a thin and even layer. Cook, undisturbed, for about 30 seconds.

4 Hold the pan handle, ease a fish slice under the pancake, then quickly lift and flip it over. Make sure the pancake is lying flat against the base of the pan with no folds, then cook for another 30 seconds before turning out on to a warm plate. Keep warm. Continue with the rest of the batter, serving the pancakes as they cook or stack on to a plate. You can freeze the pancakes for 1 month, wrapped in cling film, or make them up to a day ahead.

· ·
PER PANCAKE 107 kcals, protein 4g, carbs 12g, fat 5g, sat fat 1g, fibre none, sugar 2g, salt 0.2g

One-pan English breakfast

For a vegetarian version, swap the chipolatas for veggie sausages, omit the bacon and add more mushrooms.

 20 minutes 4

- 4 good-quality pork chipolatas
- 4 rashers smoked back bacon
- 140g/5oz button mushrooms
- 6 eggs, beaten
- 8 cherry tomatoes, halved
- handful grated cheese (optional)
- 1 tbsp snipped chives

1 Heat the grill to high. Heat a medium non-stick frying pan, add the chipolatas and fry for 3 minutes. Add the bacon and cook, turning occasionally, until it starts to crisp – about 5 minutes. Tip in the mushrooms and continue to cook for a further 3–5 minutes. Drain off any excess fat and move the ingredients around the pan so they are evenly spread out.

2 Season the eggs, then add them to the pan, swirling them to fill the spaces. Gently move the egg around with a fork for 2 minutes over a low–medium heat until it is beginning to set.

3 Scatter over the tomatoes and cheese (if using), then grill for 2 minutes until set. Sprinkle with the chives, cut into wedges and serve.

PER SERVING 349 kcals, protein 25g, carbs 4g, fat 26g, sat fat 8g, fibre 1g, sugar 2g, salt 2.27g

Hash browns with mustard & smoked salmon

· ·

This brilliant brunch is sensational, whatever the time of year. Try adding baby leaf spinach or peppery watercress to complement the delicious flavours.

 20 minutes 4

- 1 large potato (about 350g/12oz), washed
- 1 tbsp plain flour
- 1 tbsp wholegrain mustard or horseradish sauce
- knob butter
- 1 tbsp sunflower oil
- 4 slices smoked salmon
- snipped chives, to garnish
- soured cream or crème fraîche, to serve

1 Grate the unpeeled potato on to a clean tea towel. Bring up the edges of the towel, then squeeze it over the sink to remove any excess liquid from the potatoes. Tip into a bowl and add the flour and mustard or horseradish. Season well and mix together.

2 Divide the mixture into eight balls and flatten between your hands. Heat a large frying pan with the butter and oil, then add the potatoes to the pan. Cook for 2–3 minutes on each side, over a medium heat, until golden.

3 Stack a couple of hash browns on each serving plate and top with a slice of smoked salmon. Serve with soured cream or crème fraîche alongside and garnish with chives.

· ·
PER SERVING 153 kcals, protein 9g, carbs 18g, fat 6g, sat fat 2g, fibre 1g, sugar 1g, salt 1.61g

Pistou soup

. . . .

The pesto and beans can be prepared a day in advance and kept covered with cling film in the fridge. This high-fibre soup delivers two of your 5-a-day.

 45 minutes   8

- 2 tbsp olive oil
- 1 onion, finely chopped
- 2 carrots, peeled and finely chopped
- 2 celery sticks, finely chopped
- 1 small fennel bulb, trimmed and finely chopped
- 250g/9oz each turnip, celeriac and parsnip, peeled, cored and finely chopped
- 140g/5oz frozen peas
- 140g/5oz canned haricot beans, drained and rinsed
- grated Parmesan and croutons, to garnish

FOR THE PESTO
- large bunch basil
- 1 garlic clove
- 100ml/3½fl oz extra virgin olive oil

1 Heat the oil in a large pan and sweat the onion, carrots, celery, fennel, turnip, celeriac and parsnip for 5–10 minutes. Pour over 1.6 litres/2¾ pints boiling water, season and simmer for 10–15 minutes, until the vegetables are tender. At the last moment, add the peas and the beans, and cook for a further 1 minute. Taste and check the seasoning.

2 Meanwhile, make the pesto sauce. Blanch the basil leaves in boiling water for 5 seconds then remove and cool under cold running water. Pat dry and purée all the pesto ingredients in a liquidiser. Taste and season, then reserve. Keep in the fridge until required.

3 When ready to serve, pour the soup into a large, warmed tureen and top with some of the pesto sauce. Put Parmesan and croûtons on the table so everyone can help themselves.

. . . .

PER SERVING 201 kcals, protein 4g, carbs 13g, fat 15g, sat fat 2g, fibre 7g, sugar 7g, salt 0.15g

Garlic mushrooms on toast

These creamy mushrooms also make a quick and tempting lunch or a speedy supper – choose granary baguettes for their lower GI.

 15 minutes 4

- 2 tsp vegetable oil
- 500g pack button mushrooms, halved
- 2 garlic cloves, crushed
- ½ x 300g tub garlic and herb soft cheese
- 150ml/¼ pint hot vegetable stock
- 2 small baguettes, sliced open and halved

1 Heat the oil in a large frying pan, then tip in the mushrooms and garlic, and cook for 3 minutes. Stir in the soft cheese and the stock, and simmer for 2 minutes.
2 Lightly toast the baguettes, top with the warm mushroom mix and a grinding of black pepper, and serve.

PER SERVING 355 kcals, protein 11g, carbs 37g, fat 19g, sat fat 10g, fibre 3g, sugar 3g, salt 1.47g

Classic cheese soufflé

This veggie classic stands the test of time and is still a real showstopper.

🕐 45 minutes   4

- 50g/2oz butter, plus extra for greasing
- 25g/1oz breadcrumbs
- 50g/2oz plain flour
- 1 tsp mustard powder
- 300ml/½ pint milk
- 4 eggs
- 100g/4oz extra-strong Cheddar, grated

1 Heat oven to 200C/180C fan/gas 6. Put a baking sheet on the middle shelf. Butter a 15cm soufflé dish and sprinkle in the breadcrumbs.

2 Melt the butter in a pan. Stir in the flour and mustard powder. Gradually stir in the milk, mixing thoroughly before adding more. Stir continuously until the liquid thickens, then transfer to a bowl. Separate the eggs, putting the whites in a clean bowl. Stir the yolks into the sauce with the cheese.

3 Whisk the egg whites until peaks form. With a metal spoon, gently fold the whipped whites into the white sauce.

4 Spoon the mixture into the prepared soufflé dish. Run a cutlery knife around the edge to create a 'top hat' effect. Put the soufflé dish on the baking sheet and bake the soufflé for 25–30 minutes or until the top is golden, risen and has a slight wobble. Serve immediately.

PER SERVING 402 kcals, protein 19g, carbs 18g, fat 29g, sat fat 15g, fibre 1g, sugar 4g, salt 1.02g

Orange, walnut & blue-cheese salad

Crunchy, fruity, zingy and on the table in 15 minutes – this recipe ticks all the boxes for a refreshing and tasty starter or a light lunch.

 15 minutes   4

- 2 x 100g bags rocket, watercress and spinach salad
- 2 oranges
- 1 tbsp walnut oil
- 85g/3oz walnut pieces, roughly chopped
- 140g/5oz blue cheese, crumbled

1 Empty the bags of salad into a large bowl. Peel the oranges over a small bowl to catch the juices; then, over the same bowl, cut the segments from the pith and reserve.

2 Whisk the walnut oil into the orange juice, season and pour over the salad leaves. Toss the salad, then arrange on a large platter. Scatter over the orange segments, walnuts and blue cheese to serve.

PER SERVING 356 kcals, protein 14g, carbs 8g, fat 30g, sat fat 10g, fibre 3g, sugar 8g, salt 0.8g

Griddled aubergines with yogurt & mint

This dish is low in saturated fat, sugar and salt, and incredibly versatile – serve as a starter, an accompaniment to meat or as a sandwich filling.

 45 minutes 4

- 4 small aubergines, sliced into 1cm/½in thick rounds
- 2 tbsp olive oil
- 150g pot natural yogurt
- juice ½ lemon
- 2 garlic cloves, crushed
- 1 small bunch mint leaves, coarsely chopped

1 Drizzle the aubergine slices with olive oil and a little salt and pepper, and toss in a bowl. Heat a griddle pan until hot and cook the slices on both sides until soft and lightly charred; you'll need to do this in batches. Leave to cool slightly on a serving plate.

2 Meanwhile, mix the yogurt with the lemon juice, garlic and most of the mint in a bowl. Season the mixture to taste. Drizzle the yogurt mixture over the griddled aubergine, scatter with the remaining mint and serve at room temperature.

PER SERVING 105 kcals, protein 4g, carbs 8g, fat 7g, sat fat 1g, fibre 4g, sugar 6g, salt 0.33g

Cumin roast peppers, tomatoes & olives
· · · · · · · · · · · · · · · · · · · ·

Roasting brings out the best in lots of vegetables, but peppers surely top the list. This [is] also perfect as a low-fat, sugar and salt side dish to accompany roast chicken or fish

 40 minutes   6

- 4 red peppers, deseeded and cut into chunks
- 3 tbsp olive oil
- 2 x 300g packs cherry tomatoes on the vine (or use smallish tomatoes and halve them)
- 1 tsp cumin seed
- 100g/4oz pitted fat green olives

1 Heat oven to 200C/180C fan/gas 6. Put the peppers in a medium-sized roasting tin (or an ovenproof frying pan will do) and splash with 2 tablespoons of the oil. Season generously, then roast for about 20 minutes or until softened a little.

2 Remove the tin from the oven, sit the bunches of tomatoes among the peppers, scatter the cumin over everything, then drizzle with the rest of the oil. Season again, then return to the oven and roast for about 10 minutes or until the tomato skins have split. Toss the olives through just before serving, either warm or cold.

· ·
PER SERVING 116 kcals, protein 2g, carbs 10g, fat 8g, sat fat 1g, fibre 3g, sugar 9g, salt 1g

Roasted swede with Parmesan

. . . .

At Sunday lunch, serve up something other than roast potatoes with these tasty, cheesy chunks of swede.

 45 minutes 4

- 1 large swede (about 750g/1lb 10oz), peeled and cut into chips
- 1 tbsp olive oil, plus extra for greasing
- 50g/2oz Parmesan, grated
- 1 tbsp chopped rosemary leaves
- knob butter
- 2 garlic cloves, peeled

1 Heat oven to 220C/200C fan/gas 7. Tip the swede, olive oil, 40g/1½oz of the Parmesan and the rosemary leaves into a shallow roasting tin. Season and toss well, arranging in one layer. Sprinkle over the remaining Parmesan, dot with butter, then add the garlic cloves.

2 Roast for 30–35 minutes until crisp and golden, turning halfway through cooking.

. . . .

PER SERVING 155 kcals, protein 6g, carbs 10g, fat 10g, sat fat 4g, fibre 4g, sugar 9g, salt 0.34g

Spinach with coconut

The addition of coconut makes this a typically southern-Indian dish. Fresh coconut is a rich source of nutrients and of fibre, which helps regulate blood-sugar levels.

 45 minutes 6

- 50g/2oz yellow split peas or red split lentils
- 2 tbsp vegetable oil
- 1 tsp mustard seeds
- 5 curry leaves (optional)
- 2 small thin red chillies
- 1 small onion, chopped
- 250g/9oz spinach leaves, shredded
- ½ fresh coconut, flesh grated

1 In a pan of boiling water, cook the split peas for about 25 minutes until they are tender but still keep their shape. Or, if you are using lentils, cook them for 15–20 minutes.

2 Meanwhile, heat the vegetable oil in a large pan, then add the mustard seeds, curry leaves (if using), whole red chillies and chopped onion, and fry for 5 minutes.

3 Wash and drain the shredded spinach. Drain the split peas or lentils, then add to the pan of spices with the grated coconut, and toss over the heat for another 5 minutes. Add the spinach and, when it has wilted, season and serve.

PER SERVING 136 kcals, protein 4g, carbs 6g, fat 11g, sat fat 6g, fibre 2g, sugar 2g, salt 0.16g

Spiced rice & beans

This is a version of an Indian dish called kitchari and a great storecupboard supper. The tomato topping adds a refreshing tang to the spicy rice.

 40 minutes 4

- 200g/8oz basmati rice
- 2 tbsp oil
- 1 onion, chopped
- 2cm/¾in piece ginger, chopped
- 2 garlic cloves, finely chopped
- 1 green chilli, deseeded and finely chopped
- 1 tsp each cumin and mustard seeds
- 400g can black-eyed beans/peas, drained and rinsed
- 2 bay leaves
- 1 cinnamon stick
- 1 tsp ground turmeric
- 2 tbsp pumpkin seeds, plain or toasted, to garnish

TOMATO TOPPING
- 300g/11oz tomatoes, chopped
- 1 tsp grated ginger
- ½ red onion, finely chopped

1 Rinse the rice several times in cold water until the water runs clear. Drain well. Heat the oil in a large pan, add the onion and ginger, and fry for 5 minutes until the onion is lightly coloured. Stir in the garlic, chilli, cumin and mustard seeds, and fry for 1 minute.

2 Tip the rice and beans/peas into the pan, and mix well. Add 600ml/1 pint water, the bay leaves, cinnamon stick, turmeric and a little salt. Bring to the boil, then reduce the heat, cover and cook gently for about 15 minutes until the rice is tender.

3 Meanwhile, mix together the tomatoes, ginger and red onion for the topping with plenty of freshly ground black pepper and a little salt. Serve the rice and beans/peas in warmed bowls topped with the tomato mixture and sprinkled with pumpkin seeds.

PER SERVING 332 kcals, protein 11g, carbs 56g, fat 9g, sat fat 1g, fibre 3g, sugar 3g, salt 0.58g

Sweetcorn salsa

This vivid, vegetarian dish can be thrown together in next to no time. The fresh, sweet tasting corn works perfectly with the jalapeño, coriander, lime and feta.

 20 minutes 4

- 4 fresh corn cobs
- 2 vine tomatoes, chopped
- ½ red onion, chopped
- 1 red pepper, deseeded and chopped
- 1 avocado, stoned, peeled and chopped
- 1 jalapeño pepper, deseeded and finely chopped
- handful coriander leaves, roughly chopped
- juice 3 limes
- 75g/2½oz feta

1 Boil the corn for about 5 minutes or until tender. Run under cold water and drain thoroughly. Cut the corn off the cob and put in a large serving bowl.
2 Add the tomatoes, onion, red pepper, avocado, jalapeño pepper, coriander, lime juice and some seasoning, and mix well. Crumble the feta over the sweetcorn salsa to serve.

PER SERVING 227 kcals, protein 8g, carbs 20g, fat 13g, sat fat 4g, fibre 4g, sugar 7g, salt 0.7g

Spicy falafels

Falafels are a tasty way to enjoy low-GI chickpeas. This recipe can be easily multiplied to feed a crowd or to serve as nibbles.

 20 minutes 6

- 2 tbsp sunflower or vegetable oil
- 1 small onion, finely chopped
- 1 garlic clove, crushed
- 400g can chickpeas, drained and rinsed
- 1 tsp ground cumin
- 1 tsp ground coriander (or use more cumin)
- handful parsley leaves, chopped, or 1 tsp dried mixed herbs
- 1 egg, beaten
- wholemeal pitta, green salad and sliced tomatoes, to serve

1 Heat 1 tablespoon of the oil in a large pan, then fry the onion and garlic over a low heat for 5 minutes or until softened.
2 Tip the onion mix into a large bowl with the chickpeas and spices, then mash together with a fork or potato masher until the chickpeas are totally broken down. Stir in the parsley or dried herbs, and add some seasoning to taste. Add the egg, then squish the mixture together with your hands.
3 Mould the mixture into six balls, then flatten into patties. Heat the remaining oil in the pan and fry the falafels on a medium heat for 3 minutes on each side, or until golden brown and firm. Serve hot or cold stuffed into wholemeal pitta breads with some green salad and sliced tomatoes.

PER SERVING (2 FALAFELS) 210 kcals, protein 10g, carbs 16g, fat 12g, sat fat 2g, fibre 4g, sugar 2g, salt 0.5

Best bean spread

Versatile and tasty, this spread is brilliant stuffed into pitta with fresh veg, such as carrots, celery or cucumber sticks and cherry tomatoes, or use in place of houmous.

 10 minutes 4

- 410g can butter beans, drained and rinsed
- 2 tbsp olive oil
- 2 tbsp lemon juice
- 125g pack low-fat garlic and herb soft cheese
- wholemeal pitta or veggie sticks, to serve

1 Put the butter beans into a food processor, then pour in the olive oil and lemon juice. Add a pinch of salt and some freshly ground black pepper. Whizz together to make a smooth paste.

2 Add the garlic and herb cheese, blend until smooth, then chill until ready to eat. Alternatively, put into a sealable container and keep in the fridge for up to 3 days.

3 Serve stuffed into wholemeal pitta or use as a dip for veggie snacks.

PER SERVING 151 kcals, protein 6g, carbs 9g, fat 11g, sat fat 4g, fibre 3g, sugar 2g, salt 0.97g

Red-onion & Indian-spiced houmous

Houmous makes a perfect snack or starter, or serve it with oatcakes as a light lunch. This recipe is spiked with gentle spices to make it deliciously different.

 25 minutes 2

- 2 tbsp olive oil
- 1 red onion, thinly sliced
- 1 tsp each cumin and coriander seeds
- ½ tsp fennel seeds
- 400g can chickpeas, drained and rinsed
- juice ½ lemon
- 1 tbsp tahini paste
- 2 tsp finely chopped coriander leaves
- pitta bread, to serve

1 In a non-stick pan, heat 1 tablespoon of the oil, then fry the onion until soft and lightly browned. Remove from the heat and set aside to cool while you prepare the rest of the ingredients.

2 Toast the spices in a dry pan over a low heat for a couple of minutes, then remove from the heat and grind to make a powder. In a food processor, blitz together the chickpeas, lemon juice, tahini, spices, some salt, the coriander and the onion until smooth.

3 Tip into a serving bowl and dress with the remaining olive oil. Serve with pitta, if you like.

PER SERVING 314 kcals, protein 11g, carbs 25g, fat 20g, sat fat 2g, fibre 6g, sugar 4g, salt 0.69g

Red-lentil & sweet-potato pâté

With its natural sweetness this low-fat pâté is a great option for keeping in the fridge for a home-from-school snack or to pack into a lunchbox with some crispy veg sticks.

🕐 40 minutes, plus chilling   🥧 4

- 1 tbsp olive oil, plus extra for drizzling
- ½ onion, finely chopped
- 1 tsp smoked paprika, plus a little extra to dust
- 1 small sweet potato, peeled and diced
- 140g/5oz red split lentils
- 3 thyme sprigs, leaves chopped, plus a few extra leaves to garnish (optional)
- 500ml/18fl oz low-sodium vegetable stock
- 1 tsp red wine vinegar
- pitta bread and vegetable sticks, to serve

1 Heat the oil in a large pan, add the onion and cook slowly until soft and golden. Tip in the paprika and cook for a further 2 minutes, then add the sweet potato, lentils, thyme and stock. Bring to a simmer, then cook for 20 minutes or until the sweet potato and lentils are tender.

2 Add the vinegar and some seasoning, and roughly mash the mixture until you get a texture you like. Chill for 1 hour, then drizzle with the extra olive oil, dust with the extra paprika and sprinkle with thyme leaves, if you like. Serve with pitta bread and vegetable sticks.

PER SERVING 200 kcals, protein 9g, carbs 28g, fat 5g, sat fat 1g, fibre 3g, sugar 5g, salt 0.4g

Ricotta & spring-onion dip

Taking only minutes to make, this dip is great for a nibble before dinner or served at lunch with celery, cucumber sticks and some toasted wholemeal bread.

🕐 5 minutes   🥧 6, as a nibble

- 140g/5oz ricotta
- 3 spring onions, roughly chopped
- juice and zest ½ lemon
- 50g/2oz soured cream, crème fraîche or natural yogurt

1 Whizz the ricotta with most of the chopped spring onions and the lemon juice and zest, soured cream, crème fraîche or natural yogurt and some seasoning.

2 Keep chilled until ready to eat, then scatter with the remaining sliced spring onions before serving with toasted bread.

PER SERVING 72 kcals, protein 3g, carbs 1g, fat 6g, sat fat 4g, fibre none, sugar 1g, salt 0.1g

Spicy chickpeas

Get the whole family snacking on this healthier alternative to salted peanuts.

 30 minutes 4

- 400g can chickpeas, drained, rinsed and dried
- 1 tsp vegetable oil
- 1 tbsp chilli powder

1 Heat oven to 180C/160C fan/gas 4. Tip the chickpeas into a bowl with the vegetable oil and chilli powder, and mix until the chickpeas are coated with chilli. Transfer to a baking sheet, spread out the chickpeas, then cook for 25 minutes. Remove from the oven and allow to cool.

2 Sprinkle with sea salt before serving.

PER SERVING 80 kcals, protein 5g, carbs 10g, fat 2g, sat fat none, fibre 3g, sugar trace, salt 0.41g

Spiced-chilli popcorn

A guilt-free treat! This snack is sure to fill you up.

 13 minutes 5

- 1 pouch natural microwave popcorn or 100g/4oz popcorn kernels
- 1 tsp chilli flakes
- 1 tsp cracked black pepper
- 2 tsp ground mixed spice

1 Heat oven to 200C/180C fan/gas 6. Pop the natural microwave popcorn pouch (or popcorn kernels) according to the pack instructions.

2 Meanwhile, mix together the chilli flakes, cracked black pepper and mixed spice. Toss the popcorn with the spice mix, then tip on to a large baking sheet and put in the oven for 5 minutes until the corn is crisp and the spice are fragrant.

3 Sprinkle with a pinch of salt and eat warm or once cooled. Will keep in an airtight container for up to a week.

PER SERVING 128 kcals, protein 2g, carbs 11g, fat 9g, sat fat 1g, fibre none, sugar trace, salt 0.02g

Houmous & avocado with tomato salad

You can prepare this delicious salad ahead, but rub the cut and stoned avocado with a little lemon juice if you're not planning to tuck in straight away.

 5 minutes 2

- 1 small red onion, sliced
- 2 tomatoes, chopped
- handful pitted black olives
- squeeze lemon juice
- olive oil, for drizzling
- 1 avocado
- 2 tbsp houmous
- toasted crusty bread, to serve

1 Combine the onion, tomatoes and olives with the lemon juice. Drizzle with oil and season to taste.

2 Halve and stone the avocado, then spoon the houmous into the space where the stone was. Scatter with the tomato salad, drizzle with a little more oil and serve with toasted crusty bread.

PER SERVING 436 kcals, protein 5g, carbs 9g, fat 43g, sat fat 5g, fibre 7g, sugar 5g, salt 0.46g

Halloumi kebabs with thyme & lemon baste

With a full-on flavour, these kebabs are delicious served with a crisp green salad or warm flatbreads.

 25 minutes 4

- 2 medium courgettes
- 1 large red onion
- 250g/9oz low-fat halloumi, cut into 16 chunks
- 16 cherry tomatoes
- warm flatbread, to serve

FOR THE BASTE
- 1 tbsp olive oil
- 2 tbsp lemon juice
- 2 tsp thyme leaves (preferably lemon thyme)
- 1 tsp Dijon mustard

1 Heat the barbecue or grill to hot. Halve the courgettes lengthways, then thickly slice. Cut the onion into wedges and separate into pieces. Thread the halloumi, cherry tomatoes, courgette and onion chunks on to eight skewers.

2 To make the baste, mix together the olive oil, lemon juice, thyme, mustard and a little seasoning, to taste.

3 Arrange the kebabs on the rack. Brush with the baste, stirring it first to make sure the ingredients are blended. Cook for 4–5 minutes, turning often, until the cheese begins to turn golden and the vegetables are just tender. Serve while still hot with warm flatbreads, if you like.

PER SERVING 225 kcals, protein 18g, carbs 7g, fat 13g, sat fat 7g, fibre 2g, sugar 6g, salt 1.8g

Cracked-wheat & fennel salad

· · · · · · · · · · · · · · · · · · · ·

A delicious combination of roasted fennel and zesty orange served on a bed of herby, low GI bulghar wheat.

 45 minutes   4

- 250g/9oz bulghar wheat
- 3 fennel bulbs, cut into wedges
- 4 tbsp olive oil
- zest and juice 2 oranges
- 4 tbsp chopped flat-leaf parsley
- 2 tbsp chopped mint leaves
- 4 plum tomatoes, cut into wedges
- 140g/5oz pitted mixed olives, drained
- 100g/4oz rocket leaves

1 Heat oven to 200C/180C fan/gas 6. Put the bulghar wheat in a large bowl, then cover with 1 litre/1¾ pints boiling water, then cover with cling film and allow to stand for 30 minutes. Meanwhile, put the fennel in a large roasting tin, drizzle with the olive oil and season. Add the orange zest and half the orange juice, and roast in the oven for 35 minutes until softened and slightly charred.

2 Drain the bulghar wheat, add the parsley and mint and remaining orange juice. Combine well and season to taste. Put the tomatoes, olives and rocket in a large bowl, add the roasted fennel with the pan juices and toss well.

3 Divide the bulghar wheat among four serving plates, top with the fennel and tomato mixture and serve.

· ·

PER SERVING 426 kcals, protein 10g, carbs 54g, fat 17g, sat fat 2g, fibre 8g, sugar 8g, salt 2.1g

Portobello burgers

Topped with melting, garlicky Gruyère, these big, juicy low-fat burgers will appeal to everyone.

 20 minutes 4

- 4 portobello or field mushrooms, stalks trimmed
- 1 tsp sunflower oil
- 50g/2oz Gruyère, grated
- 1 garlic clove, crushed
- 1 tbsp butter, softened
- 4 ciabatta or burger buns, split and toasted
- lettuce, tomatoes and sliced red onion, to serve

1 Heat grill to high. Rub the mushrooms with the oil and set on a baking sheet. Grill for 3 minutes on each side until cooked, but still firm.
2 Mix the cheese, garlic, butter and some seasoning in a bowl, then spoon into the mushrooms. Grill until the cheese melts, then stuff into the toasted buns with the salad and serve.

PER SERVING 228 kcals, protein 11g, carbs 23g, fat 11g, sat fat 5g, fibre 3g, sugar 1g, salt 1.05g

Stuffed sweet peppers

These peppers have a fabulous flavour when cooked on the barbecue. To increase their smokiness, cook them with the barbecue lid on.

 30 minutes 4

- 4 long sweet red peppers, halved lengthways through the stalk and deseeded
- 1 tbsp olive oil, plus extra to drizzle (optional)
- 2 x 125g mozzarella, sliced
- 2 tbsp pitted black olives, chopped
- 1 tbsp chopped oregano leaves
- 2 garlic cloves, crushed

1 Heat the barbecue or griddle pan to hot. Rub the outside of the peppers all over with the olive oil.
2 Stuff the peppers with the mozzarella, olives, oregano and garlic, and drizzle with a touch more olive oil, if you like.
3 Pop on the barbecue or into the pan, stuffed-side up, for 12–15 minutes until the peppers are nicely charred (or roast in a roasting tin in the oven at 220C/200C fan/gas 7 for the same amount of time). Serve straight away.

PER SERVING 282 kcals, protein 13g, carbs 8g, fat 22g, sat fat 9g, fibre 2g, sugar 7g, salt 0.73g

Superfood pasta salad

The aromatic Asian-style sesame, lime and ginger dressing in this recipe goes brilliantly with pasta.

 20 minutes   4

- 300g/11oz wholewheat penne
- 250g/9oz frozen soya beans
- 250g pack green beans, trimmed and halved
- 1 tsp sesame oil
- 1 tbsp light soy sauce
- small knob ginger, grated
- juice 1 lime
- 50g/2oz alfalfa sprouts or cress
- 2 carrots, grated
- 1 small bunch coriander, leaves roughly chopped

1 Cook the pasta according to the pack instructions, adding the soya beans and green beans 3 minutes before the end of cooking. Drain, tip into a colander, then cool quickly under cold running water.
2 Whisk together the oil, soy sauce, ginger and lime juice in a large bowl, then tip in the pasta, cooked beans, alfalfa sprouts or cress, carrots and coriander. Toss the salad well, then serve.

PER SERVING 379 kcals, protein 20g, carbs 63g, fat 7g, sat fat 1g, fibre 12g, sugar 8g, salt 0.96g

Spanish spinach omelette

A large omelette makes a great family supper. This one is ideal for all ages, as it's a good source of folic acid, low in saturated fat, sugar and salt.

 30 minutes · 8 wedges

- 400g bag spinach leaves
- 3 tbsp olive oil
- 1 large onion, finely sliced
- 10 eggs
- 2 large peeled and cooked potatoes, thickly sliced

1 Tip the spinach into a large colander and bring a kettleful of water to the boil. Slowly pour the boiling water over the spinach until wilted, then cool the leaves under cold water. Squeeze all the liquid out of the spinach, chop roughly and set aside.

2 Heat the oil in a grill-proof non-stick frying pan and gently cook the onion for 10 minutes until soft.

3 Heat grill to high. While the onion is cooking, beat the eggs together in a large bowl and season with salt and pepper. Stir the spinach and the potatoes into the pan, then pour in the eggs. Cook, stirring occasionally until nearly set, then grill for a few minutes until just set all the way through. Flip on to a board and cut into wedges to serve.

PER WEDGE 209 kcals, protein 12g, carbs 11g, fat 13g, sat fat 3g, fibre 2g, sugar 2g, salt 0.46g

Healthy egg & chips

It's amazing what you can make with just a few ingredients. This recipe is a healthy option – low in fat, sugar and salt and makes its way to the table with minimum effort

🕐 40 minutes   🥧 4

- 500g/1lb 2oz potatoes, diced
- 2 shallots, sliced
- 1 tbsp olive oil
- 2 tsp dried oregano or 1 tsp chopped leaves
- 200g/7oz small mushrooms
- 4 eggs

1 Heat oven to 200C/180C fan/gas 6. Tip the potatoes and shallots into a large non-stick roasting tin, drizzle with the oil, sprinkle over the oregano, then mix everything together well. Bake in the oven for 15 minutes, add the mushrooms, then cook for a further 10 minute until the potatoes are browned and tender.

2 Make four gaps in the vegetables then crack an egg into each space. Return to the oven for 3–4 minutes or until the eggs are cooked to your liking and ready to serve.

PER SERVING 218 kcals, protein 11g, carbs 22g, fat 10g, sat fat 2g, fibre 2g, sugar 1g, salt 0.24g

Courgette & ricotta tart

Topping this tart with ricotta and green veg makes the dish much lighter than you expect. Serve with a green salad to give plenty of complementary crunch.

 50 minutes   6

- 2 tbsp olive oil
- 2 courgettes, thinly sliced
- 250g tub ricotta
- 2 eggs, beaten with a fork
- small handful basil leaves, shredded
- pinch grated nutmeg
- 1 tbsp grated Parmesan (or vegetarian alternative)
- 1 garlic clove, crushed
- 320g pack ready-rolled puff pastry
- flour, for dusting
- green salad, to serve

1 Heat oven to 200C/180C fan/gas 6. Heat the oil in a frying pan. Cook the courgettes until golden around the edges, then remove from the pan and set aside. Mix together the ricotta, eggs, most of the basil, the nutmeg, Parmesan and garlic in a bowl.
2 Unroll the pastry on a lightly floured surface – roll it out lightly to make it a little thinner. Lay it on a baking sheet.
3 Spread the pastry with the ricotta mix, leaving a small border around the edge, then press the courgette slices into the ricotta. Bring the pastry sides up over the edge of the filling and pinch so that none seeps out the sides.
4 Bake for 30 minutes until the tart is puffed up and golden. Serve warm, scattered with the remaining basil, and with a green salad alongside.

PER SLICE 341 kcals, protein 11g, carbs 21g, fat 24g, sat fat 11g, fibre 1g, sugar 2g, salt 0.6g

Chargrilled courgette & salmon salad

Double the ingredients to make a light main course for four people. Salmon is an oily fish, rich in heart-friendly omega-3 fats.

 30 minutes  2

- 4 tbsp fruity olive oil
- juice 1 lemon
- 2 tsp dried herbes de Provence
- 1 garlic clove, crushed
- 8 baby courgettes (200g pack), each cut in half lengthways
- 2 skinless salmon fillets (about 300g/10oz total), each cut into 3 strips
- 85g bag herb salad, to serve

FOR THE DRESSING
- 3 tbsp fruity olive oil
- 1 tbsp lemon juice
- 1 tsp grainy mustard
- 2 tbsp chopped tarragon leaves

1 First make the dressing. Measure the ingredients into a jug or screw-topped jar, season to taste, then whisk or shake to mix. Set aside.

2 Now mix the olive oil, lemon juice, herbs and garlic in a bowl with salt and pepper to taste. Toss the courgette halves in this marinade until they're thoroughly coated.

3 Heat a ridged griddle pan until very hot but not smoking, or use a good non-stick frying pan instead (but you won't get attractive dark stripes). Sear the courgettes in batches for 2–3 minutes on each side until just softened, with dark stripes. Remove and set aside.

4 Put the strips of salmon into the remaining marinade in the dish and toss to coat, then chargrill on the griddle pan for 1–2 minutes on each side until just cooked through.

5 To serve, divide the salad leaves between two plates and lay the courgettes and salmon on top. Re-whisk the dressing and drizzle it over everything. Serve at once.

PER SERVING 635 kcals, protein 31g, carbs 5g, fat 55g, sat fat 9g, fibre 1g, sugar 2g, salt 0.27g

Hot-smoked salmon, double-cress & potato-salad platter

This salad platter is the ideal choice when feeding guests. Prepare all the elements in advance (except the avocado, or it will go brown) then assemble and serve.

 1 hour 10 minutes   8

- 400g/14oz small new potatoes
- 100g/4oz green beans, trimmed
- 12 quail's eggs
- 2 packs hot-smoked salmon (about 350g/12oz total)
- 2 avocados
- 2 x 100g bags watercress
- 1 chicory head, broken into leaves
- 5 spring onions, trimmed and sliced
- 1 pot mustard cress, trimmed

FOR THE DRESSING
- 1 tbsp wholegrain mustard
- 1 tsp clear honey
- 3 tbsp cider vinegar
- 8 tbsp olive oil

1 To make the dressing, whisk all the ingredients together in a bowl with some seasoning and set aside.

2 Cook the potatoes in plenty of boiling water for 10 minutes until just tender. Drain, cool slightly, then slice. Set aside.

3 Meanwhile, blanch the beans in boiling water for 4 minutes until cooked, drain, plunge into iced water, then drain again. Boil the quail's eggs for 3 minutes. Drain, put under cold water, then peel and halve. Flake the salmon into large chunks into a bowl. Just before serving, halve, peel and slice the avocados.

4 This is a layered rather than a tossed salad, so start by scattering watercress and chicory over a platter. Scatter different handfuls at a time of all the other ingredients (but not the mustard cress). Drizzle over two-thirds of the dressing, then strew the mustard cress to finish. Serve with the remaining dressing on the side.

PER SERVING 315 kcals, protein 15g, carbs 11g, fat 24g, sat fat 3g, fibre 3g, sugar 2g, salt 1.3g

Spicy chicken salad with broccoli

· ·

Try this spicy dish for lunch, or add some cooked egg noodles to make a more substantial salad or light supper.

 25 minutes   4

- 2 broccoli heads, cut into florets
- 2 tbsp olive oil
- 5 shallots or 1 large onion, finely sliced
- 2 red chillies, deseeded and sliced
- 2 garlic cloves, sliced
- handful pitted black olives
- 4 roast chicken breasts, sliced
- 4 tbsp reduced-salt soy sauce

1 Steam the broccoli for 4 minutes until just tender, tip into a large bowl, then season. Meanwhile, heat the oil in a pan and fry the shallots or onion for 2 minutes. Add the chillies and garlic, then cook for a further 4 minutes until softened. Lift out the shallots, chillies and garlic with a slotted spoon, then mix with the broccoli, olives and chicken in a bowl.

2 Add the soy sauce to the pan, warm it over a medium heat, then pour it over the salad. Eat warm or cold.

· ·
PER SERVING 298 kcals, protein 42g, carbs 4g, fat 12g, sat fat 2g, fibre 3g, sugar 3g, salt 2.3g

Lemon & rosemary pork with chickpea salad

· ·

Ring the changes by making this dish with chicken breasts, or swapping the lemon for orange. Thyme makes a good substitute for the rosemary too.

🕐 30 minutes, plus marinating   4

- 1 tbsp olive oil
- 2 tsp finely chopped rosemary
- 4 garlic cloves, crushed
- juice and zest ½ lemon
- 4 boneless pork steaks, trimmed of fat
- 1 red onion, finely sliced
- 2 tbsp sherry vinegar
- 2 x 400g cans chickpeas, drained and rinsed
- 110g bag mixed salad leaves

1 Mix the olive oil, rosemary, garlic, lemon juice and zest in a large bowl. Add the pork, turn to coat and season well. If you have time, marinate the pork in the fridge for 30 minutes.

2 Heat a large non-stick frying pan. Lift the pork out of the marinade, shaking off any excess and reserving the marinade. Cook the pork in the pan for 3–4 minutes each side or until cooked through. Leave to rest on a plate.

3 Pour the reserved marinade into the pan with the onion. Cook for 1 minute over a high heat before adding the vinegar, plus 3 tablespoons water. Bubble down for 1 minute, until the onion has softened and the dressing thickened slightly. Stir through the chickpeas, some seasoning and the resting juices from the pork. Put the salad leaves into a bowl, tip in the pan contents and gently toss. Serve immediately with the pork.

· ·

PER SERVING 396 kcals, protein 40g, carbs 23g, fat 17g, sat fat 3g, fibre 6g, sugar 3g, salt 0.90g

Steak salad with blue-cheese vinaigrette

This salad makes a special lunch for two, and the dressing adds a fabulous flavour. The steak can either be barbecued, griddled or grilled.

 25 minutes 2

- 1 fillet or rump beef steak (about 300g/11oz), trimmed
- 140g/5oz green beans, trimmed
- 1 red chicory head, leaves separated
- 25g/1oz walnuts, roughly chopped

FOR THE DRESSING
- zest and juice ½ lemon
- 1 tbsp walnut or olive oil
- 1 tbsp chopped tarragon leaves
- 1 small shallot, finely chopped
- 1 tbsp crumbled blue cheese (we used Danish blue)

1 Heat the barbecue, grill or a griddle pan. Season the steak with lots of pepper and a little salt. Cook on the barbecue, under the grill or on a griddle for 2–3 minutes each side for medium–rare, or to your liking. Let sit for 10 minutes, then cut into slices.
2 For the dressing, in a small bowl whisk together the lemon zest, juice, oil, tarragon, shallot, cheese and some salt and pepper.
3 Cook the beans in boiling water until just tender. Drain and rinse under cold water, then drain thoroughly.
4 Divide the chicory leaves between two plates and top with the beans, walnuts and steak slices. Pour the dressing over the salad just before eating.

• •
PER SERVING 390 kcals, protein 38g, carbs 5g, fat 24g, sat fat 5g, fibre 3g, sugar 3g, salt 0.42g

Chilli-bean open lasagne

An attractive way of serving lasagne. Beans help regulate blood sugar and lower cholesterol – stack the low-GI bean filling with cooked lasagne on individual plates.

 30 minutes 4

- 1 tbsp olive oil
- 1 onion, chopped
- 2 garlic cloves, crushed
- 1 red chilli, deseeded and finely sliced
- 1 small aubergine, chopped
- 1 large courgette, chopped
- 410g can borlotti beans, drained and rinsed
- 400g can chopped tomatoes
- 2 tbsp tomato purée
- 250g packet fresh lasagne sheets
- handful basil leaves, torn, plus extra to garnish
- 100g/4oz Cheddar, grated

1 Heat the oil in a large pan, then fry the onion for 2–3 minutes. Add the garlic, chilli, aubergine and courgette, then fry for a further 2–3 minutes. Stir in the beans, tomatoes, purée and some seasoning. Bring to the boil, then simmer for 5 minutes.

2 Meanwhile, cook the lasagne according to the pack instructions. Drain, then halve each sheet diagonally. Stir the torn basil leaves into the beans.

3 Put a spoonful of the bean mixture on each of four warmed serving plates, and top each with a quarter of the lasagne triangles. Top with the remaining bean mixture and a quarter of the cheese per plate. Garnish with the extra basil to serve.

PER SERVING 400 kcals, protein 17g, carbs 73g, fat 6g, sat fat 1g, fibre 11g, sugar none, salt 1.21g

Creamy mushroom spaghetti

This luxuriously creamy pasta recipe has only five ingredients and makes an ideal supper for friends.

 25 minutes 4

- 400g/14oz spaghetti
- 6 rashers streaky bacon, cut into strips
- 250g pack chestnut or button mushrooms, sliced
- 200g bag baby leaf spinach
- 100g/4oz gorgonzola or creamy blue cheese, crumbled

1 Bring a large pan of water to the boil, then cook the spaghetti according to pack instructions.

2 Meanwhile, fry the bacon in a large frying pan for 5 minutes, until starting to crisp. Tip in the mushrooms, then fry for 3 minutes until cooked. Drain the pasta and tip into the frying pan along with the spinach and cheese. Toss everything together over a low heat until the spinach has wilted and the cheese has melted. Serve immediately.

PER SERVING 505 kcals, protein 24g, carbs 75g, fat 14g, sat fat 7g, fibre 5g, sugar 4g, salt 1.8g

Artichoke, olive & lemon pasta

Stop by the deli counter and this light Mediterranean pasta will be ready in no time. Low in saturated fat, sugar and salt, it's the perfect after-work meal.

 15 minutes  4

- 400g/14oz spaghetti
- zest and juice 1 lemon
- 3 tbsp olive oil
- 50g/2oz grated Parmesan
- 100g/4oz artichoke hearts from a jar, chopped if large
- handful pitted black olives
- 100g bag wild rocket leaves

1 Cook the pasta in a large pan of boiling water according to the pack instructions.
2 While it cooks, mix together the lemon zest and juice, oil and Parmesan. Drain the pasta, reserving 3 tablespoons of the cooking water, then return the pasta to the pan with the lemon mix, cooking water, artichokes and olives. Heat through briefly, season well, stir through the rocket, then serve.

PER SERVING 528 kcals, protein 18g, carbs 76g, fat 19g, sat fat 4g, fibre 4g, sugar 4g, salt 1.05g

Spicy vegetable & quinoa laksa

If you haven't tried the healthy grain quinoa before, this is the perfect recipe to start. Actually a seed, quinoa is protein-packed and rich in iron, magnesium and fibre.

🕐 20 minutes   🥘 4

- 1 onion, sliced
- 4 tbsp korma or madras curry paste
- 1 litre/1¾ pints milk
- 750g/1lb 10oz frozen mixed vegetables
- 175g/6oz quinoa, rinsed

1 In a large pan over a medium heat, simmer the onion and the curry paste with a splash of water for 5 minutes, stirring from time to time until the onion has softened. Heat the milk in a jug in the microwave.

2 Add the vegetables and quinoa to the pan, then stir in the milk. Bring everything to the boil, simmer gently for 10 minutes or until the quinoa is cooked, and season with salt and pepper to taste.

PER SERVING 398 kcals, protein 22g, carbs 55g, fat 12g, sat fat 3g, fibre 7g, sugar 4g, salt 0.96g

Yellow-lentil & coconut curry with cauliflower

· · · · · · · · · · · · · · · · · · · ·

This curry is low-calorie and a good source of fibre and iron. Serve with basmati rice, which is rich in amylose, a starch that makes for a lower GI than other types of rice.

 1¼ hours   4

- 1 tbsp vegetable oil
- 1 onion, thinly sliced
- 2 garlic cloves, crushed
- thumb-sized piece ginger, finely chopped
- 3 tbsp curry paste
- 200g/7oz yellow lentils, rinsed
- 1.5 litres/2½ pints vegetable stock
- 3 tbsp unsweetened desiccated coconut, plus extra to sprinkle
- 1 cauliflower, broken into florets
- cooked basmati rice, to serve
- coriander leaves, to sprinkle

1 Heat the oil in a large pan, then add the onion, garlic and ginger. Cook for 5 minutes, add the curry paste, then stir-fry for 1 minute before adding the lentils, stock and coconut. Bring the mixture to the boil and simmer for 40 minutes or until the lentils are soft.
2 During the final 10 minutes of cooking, stir in the cauliflower to cook.
3 Spoon the rice into four bowls, top with the curry and sprinkle with coriander leaves and the extra coconut.

· ·
PER SERVING 356 kcals, protein 18g, carbs 33g, fat 17g, sat fat 9g, fibre 10g, sugar 9g, salt 1.4g

Crispy Greek-style pie

· · · · · · · · · · · · · · · · · · · ·

When working with filo pastry, cover it with some damp sheets of kitchen paper as you go along to stop it drying out.

 40 minutes 4

- 200g bag spinach leaves
- 175g jar sun-dried tomatoes in oil
- 100g/4oz feta, crumbled
- 2 eggs, beaten
- 250g pack filo pastry

1 Put the spinach into a pan with 2 tablespoons water. Cook until wilted. Tip into a sieve, squeeze out any excess water and chop. Chop the tomatoes (reserving the oil) and mix with the spinach, feta and eggs to make a filling.

2 Heat oven to 180C/160C fan/gas 4. Carefully unroll the filo pastry. Take a sheet of the pastry and brush liberally with some sun-dried tomato oil. Drape oil-side down in a 22cm-round loose-bottomed cake tin so that some of the pastry hangs over the side. Brush oil over another piece of pastry and put it in the tin, a little further round. Keep putting the filo sheets in the tin until you have three layers. Spoon over the filling. Pull the pastry sides into the middle; scrunch up, completely covering the filling. Brush with a little more of the reserved oil.

3 Cook the pie for 30 minutes or until the pastry is crisp and golden brown. Remove from the tin, slice into wedges and serve.

· ·

PER SERVING 260 kcals, protein 13g, carbs 23g, fat 14g, sat fat 5g, fibre 3g, sugar 5g, salt 3g

Couscous & fish in a bag

This simple, healthy recipe is packed with flavour and a great way to boost your iron intake.

 35 minutes   1

- 1 lemon
- 100g/4oz couscous, preferably whole-wheat
- 25g/1oz pine nuts, toasted
- 1 small courgette, thinly sliced
- small handful dill, leaves only, chopped
- 150ml/¼ pint strong vegetable stock
- 1 x 140g/5oz skinless haddock fillet or other white fish

1 Heat oven to 180C/160C fan/gas 4. Fold a large sheet of foil or non-stick baking paper in half and tightly fold one side to seal. Grate the lemon and mix the zest into the couscous, pine nuts, courgette and dill in a bowl. Season well, then tip into the open 'bag'. Cut the lemon in half, then cut two thin slices from one half. Juice the other half and add the juice to the stock.

2 Lay the haddock on top of the couscous, top with the lemon slices, then carefully pour over the lemony stock. Fold the remaining open sides tightly to seal. Bake for 20–25 minutes, depending on how thick your fish is, until the fish is cooked and couscous is fluffy.

PER SERVING 558 kcals, protein 41g, carbs 53g, fat 20g, sat fat 2g, fibre 2g, sugar 4g, salt 0.6g

Lemon fish with basil-bean mash

· ·

Fish is a healthy choice for the whole family. This tasty twist on fish and mushy peas is a great source of filling fibre and counts as two of your 5-a-day.

 25 minutes 4

- 4 small bunches cherry tomatoes on the vine
- 1 tbsp olive oil
- 4 x 140g/5oz chunks skinless white fish fillet
- zest 1 lemon, plus juice ½
- 480g pack frozen soya beans
- 2 garlic cloves
- bunch basil, leaves and stalks separated
- 200ml/7fl oz chicken or vegetable stock

1 Heat oven to 200C/180C fan/gas 6. Put the tomatoes on to a baking sheet, rub with a little of the oil and some seasoning, then roast for 5 minutes until the skins are starting to split. Add the fish, top with most of the lemon zest and some more seasoning, then drizzle with a little more of the oil. Roast for 8–10 minutes until the fish flakes easily.

2 Meanwhile, cook the beans in a pan of boiling water for 3 minutes until just tender. Drain, then tip into a food processor with the remaining oil, the garlic, basil stalks, lemon juice and stock, then pulse to a thick, slightly rough purée. Season to taste.

3 Divide the tomatoes and the bean mash among four plates, top with the fish, then scatter with basil leaves and the remaining lemon zest to serve.

· ·

PER SERVING 372 kcals, protein 44g, carbs 17g, fat 15g, sat fat 3g, fibre 6g, sugar 3g, salt 0.5g

Baked trout with fennel, radish & rocket salad

....

Being rich in healthy omega-3 fats, trout makes a fabulous special meal for two. The radish and rocket add a spicy crunch to complement the flavours of the fish.

🕐 35 minutes plus standing   🥧 2

- 2 whole trout, scaled and gutted
- ½ bunch thyme
- 2 lemons, 1 sliced, 1 juiced
- 2 tbsp olive oil, plus extra to drizzle
- 1 large fennel bulb, finely sliced
- 100g/4oz radishes, finely sliced
- 1 tbsp capers, chopped
- large handful rocket leaves

1 Heat oven to 200C/180C fan/gas 6. Slash the trout's skin three times on both sides, then stuff a thyme sprig into each cut. Lay the fish on a baking sheet lined with baking parchment, if you like, and fill the cavity with the lemon slices and remaining thyme sprigs. Season the fish, drizzle over the extra olive oil then bake for 15–20 minutes until cooked through.

2 Meanwhile, mix the lemon juice with the 2 tablespoons olive oil to make a dressing, then pour it over the fennel and allow it to stand for 10 minutes. Stir in the radishes and capers, and season. Mix the rocket through the fennel and radish salad. You can serve the trout whole or flake the flesh into large chunks, with the salad alongside.

....

PER SERVING 465 kcals, protein 57g, carbs 6g, fat 24g, sat fat 4g, fibre 4g, sugar 5g, salt 0.91g

Salmon with tarragon hollandaise

Treat someone special with this quick yet impressive dish, ready in just 10 minutes. Low in saturated fat, sugar and salt, it is also a good source of omega-3 and folic acid.

 15 minutes    2

- 1 tbsp olive oil
- 2 salmon fillets, skin on and scaled (about 140g/5oz each)
- 125g pack asparagus tips, ends trimmed
- 2 bunches cherry tomatoes on the vine
- 1 tbsp chopped tarragon leaves
- 150ml/¼ pint ready-made hollandaise sauce

1 Heat oven to 200C/180 fan/gas 6. Heat the oil in an ovenproof pan over a high heat. Add the salmon, skin-side down, then cook for 5 minutes until the skin is crisp.
2 Add the asparagus and vine tomatoes to the pan, then put in the oven. Cook for 7–10 minutes until the salmon is just cooked through.
3 Add the tarragon to the hollandaise sauce and stir through. Divide the asparagus between two plates and sit the salmon on top and the tomatoes alongside. Drizzle the sauce over the salmon and serve.

PER SERVING 327 kcals, protein 31g, carbs 3g, fat 22g, sat fat 4g, fibre 2g, sugar 3g, salt 0.18g

Spiced prawn & coconut pilaf

By cooking the rice separately, the pilaf stays nice and fluffy. Choose amylose-rich basmati rice over other varieties – it'll keep you fuller for longer.

 45 minutes 4

- 4 tbsp vegetable oil
- 1 tsp cumin seeds
- 1 cinnamon stick
- 3 each whole cloves and cardamom pods
- 1 onion, finely sliced
- fingertip-sized knob ginger, roughly chopped
- 2 large garlic cloves, sliced
- 2 tomatoes, quartered
- ½ tsp turmeric powder
- ¼ tsp hot chilli powder
- 1 heaped tsp ground coriander
- 300g/11oz raw peeled prawns
- 250g/9oz cooked basmati rice
- handful flaked coconut, to garnish (optional)

1 Heat the oil in a large non-stick pan, add the whole spices and, once they are sizzling, follow with the onion, frying for about 10 minutes until soft.

2 Meanwhile, make a paste using the ginger, garlic and tomatoes in a food processor. Add to the onion along with the ground spices and cook over a low heat, stirring every now and then for 15 minutes.

3 Add the prawns and cook for a couple of minutes until pink. Stir in the cooked rice with a fork, heat through and serve scattered with the coconut, if using.

PER SERVING 417 kcals, protein 19g, carbs 60g, fat 13g, sat fat 2g, fibre 1g, sugar 3g, salt 0.42g

Lemon-spiced chicken with chickpeas

· ·

The combination of cinnamon, coriander and cumin with the lemon, chickpeas and chicken makes this a perfectly balanced meal.

 20 minutes 4

- 1 tbsp sunflower oil
- 1 onion, halved and thinly sliced
- 4 boneless skinless chicken breasts, cut into chunks
- 1 cinnamon stick, broken in half
- 1 tsp each ground coriander and cumin
- zest and juice 1 lemon
- 400g can chickpeas, drained and rinsed
- 200ml/7fl oz chicken stock
- 250g bag spinach leaves

1 Heat the oil in a large frying pan with a lid, then fry the onion gently for 5 minutes. Turn up the heat and add the chicken, frying for about 3 minutes until golden.

2 Stir in the spices and lemon zest, fry for 1 more minute, then tip in the chickpeas and stock. Put the lid on and simmer for 5 minutes. Season to taste, then tip in the spinach and re-cover. Leave to wilt for 2 minutes, then stir through. Squeeze over the lemon juice just before serving.

· ·

PER SERVING 290 kcals, protein 42g, carbs 14g, fat 7g, sat fat 1g, fibre 4g, sugar 3g, salt 1.03g

Chargrilled lime chicken
· ·

A zesty, light dish that's low in saturated fat, sugar and salt. If you have time, marinate the chicken in the fridge for up to a day while the flavours work their magic.

🕐 30 minutes, plus marinating   🥧 4

- 4 boneless chicken breasts, skin on
- 1 tsp black peppercorns
- 3cm/1¼in ginger, grated
- 2 garlic cloves, crushed
- 1 tbsp light soy sauce
- zest 1 and juice 2 limes, plus lime wedges to squeeze over

1 Slash each chicken breast three times and put them in a shallow dish. Crush the peppercorns coarsely in a mortar and mix with the ginger, garlic, soy sauce, and lime zest and juice. Mix well, then pour over the chicken and leave to marinate in the fridge for at least 10 minutes, or overnight.

2 Heat a grill or griddle pan until hot, then cook the chicken for 6–8 minutes on each side until cooked through. Alternatively, you could do this on the barbecue: cook for the same length of time, but make sure the coals are not too fierce. Transfer to a serving dish, then carefully pour over any cooking juices. Serve with wedges of lime for squeezing.

· ·
PER SERVING 225 kcals, protein 37g, carbs 2g, fat 8g, sat fat 2g, fibre none, sugar 1g, salt 0.87g

Easy chicken Kievs

More subtle than a regular Kiev, yet this easy one-pan recipe doesn't compromise on flavour.

 25 minutes  4

- 4 boneless skinless chicken breasts
- 25g/1oz garlic butter, softened
- 25g/1oz breadcrumbs
- new potatoes and greens, to serve

1 Heat grill to medium. Put the chicken on a baking sheet, rub with a little butter, season and cook under the grill for 15 minutes, turning once, until cooked through.

2 Mix together the remaining garlic butter and the breadcrumbs. Remove the chicken from the grill and top each breast with a smear of the breadcrumbed butter. Return to the grill for 3–5 minutes more, until the breadcrumbs are golden and the butter melted. Serve the Kievs with their buttery juices, alongside new potatoes and greens.

PER SERVING 218 kcals, protein 34g, carbs 5g, fat 7g, sat fat 4g, fibre none, sugar none, salt 0.37g

Pork with garlicky bean mash

Low-GI pulses make this garlicky bean mash a tasty, nutritious alternative to mashed potato.

 20 minutes   1

- 1 pork steak, trimmed of fat
- 1 tbsp olive oil
- 1 small onion or shallot, chopped
- 1 garlic clove, crushed
- 410g can haricot beans in water, drained and rinsed
- 125ml/4fl oz vegetable stock
- 1 tbsp chopped coriander leaves

1 Heat grill to high. Lay the pork on a baking sheet and grill the steak for 12–15 minutes, turning once, until it is browned and cooked through.

2 Meanwhile, heat the oil in a small pan, add the onion or shallot and fry for 5 minutes until softened. Add the garlic to the pan, fry for 1 minute more, then tip in the beans and stock, and simmer for 5 minutes more. Roughly mash the beans with a potato masher or fork, then stir in the coriander. Serve the pork with the hot bean mash on the side.

PER SERVING 516 kcals, protein 46g, carbs 38g, fat 16g, sat fat 3g, fibre 16g, sugar 3g, salt 0.6g

Marinated lamb steaks with barley salad

Barley is rich in soluble fibre and has a low GI, so it helps stabilise blood-sugar levels and keeps you feeling full longer. This recipe is high in fibre and a good source of iron.

 45 minutes, plus marinating 2

- 2 tbsp olive oil
- 2 garlic cloves, finely chopped
- pinch dried chilli flakes
- small bunch mint, leaves chopped
- 2 lean lamb leg steaks (about 100g/4oz each), trimmed of any fat
- 100g/4oz pearl barley
- 200g/7oz broad beans, fresh or frozen, podded and skins removed (optional)
- 100g/4oz frozen petits pois
- 1 small red onion, finely chopped
- zest and juice 1 lemon

1 Mix together 1 tablespoon of the oil, the garlic, chilli, half the mint and some salt and black pepper. Rub the mix all over the steaks, then, if you have time, leave to marinate for up to 2 hours.

2 Cook the pearl barley in boiling salted water until tender, but not too soft, for about 20 minutes. Cook the beans and peas in the same pan for the last 2 minutes. Drain really well, then tip into a large bowl. Add the red onion, remaining mint, lemon zest and juice, remaining oil and some salt and black pepper. Toss everything together.

3 Heat a griddle or frying pan until almost smoking and cook the lamb for 4 minutes on each side for pink, or longer if you prefer your meat well done. Divide the barley salad between two plates and serve with the sliced grilled lamb, drizzled with any pan juices.

PER SERVING 522 kcals, protein 33g, carbs 57g, fat 20g, sat fat 4g, fibre 9g, sugar 5g, salt 0.14g

Quick lamb biryani

Forget the take away, invite some friends round and enjoy this simple yet tasty biryani.

 25 minutes   4

- 1 tbsp balti curry paste
- 500g/1lb 2oz lean lamb leg steak or neck fillet, cubed
- 200g/7oz basmati rice, rinsed in cold water
- 400ml/14fl oz lamb or chicken stock
- 200g/7oz spinach leaves

1 Heat a large pan with a lid, add the curry paste and sizzle for a minute until fragrant, then add the lamb and brown it on all sides. Pour in the rice and stock, and stir well. Bring to the boil, cover with a lid, then cook for 15 minutes on a medium heat or until the rice is tender.

2 Stir through the spinach, put the lid back on the pan and leave to steam, undisturbed, for 5 minutes more. Give everything a good stir and bring the dish to the table to let everyone help themselves.

PER SERVING 387 kcals, protein 32g, carbs 41g, fat 12g, sat fat 5g, fibre 1g, sugar 1g, salt 1.05g

Lamb meatball & pea pilaf

If you haven't made lamb meatballs before, experiment with this flavour-packed pilaf. For a really healthy twist, use turkey mince – a good source of protein and B vitamins.

 30 minutes 4

- 400g pack lean minced lamb
- 3 garlic cloves, crushed
- 2 tsp ground cumin
- 300g/11oz basmati rice, rinsed in cold water
- enough lamb or vegetable stock to cover the rice (from a cube is fine)
- 300g/11oz frozen peas
- zest 2 lemons, juice 1

FOR THE CUCUMBER YOGURT
- ½ cucumber, finely chopped or grated
- 150g pot mild natural yogurt
- small bunch mint, leaves chopped
- poppadoms, to serve

1 Mix the lamb with half the garlic and 1 teaspoon of the cumin, then season and shape into about 16 balls (it's easier to do if you wet your hands).

2 Heat a large frying pan with a lid then fry the meatballs for about 8 minutes until golden and cooked through. Remove from the pan to a plate, then tip in the rice and the remaining cumin and garlic. Fry for 30 seconds, stirring, then pour in enough stock to cover. Cover and simmer for 10 minutes or until almost all of the liquid is absorbed.

3 Stir in the peas, return the meatballs to the pan, then warm through for a few minutes until the peas are tender.

4 Meanwhile, mix the cucumber, yogurt and half the mint together, then season. To finish the pilaf, stir in the lemon zest and juice with some seasoning and the remaining mint. Serve with a good dollop of the cooling cucumber yogurt and crispy poppadoms, if you like.

PER SERVING 496 kcals, protein 33g, carbs 72g, fat 10g, sat fat 4g, fibre 4g, sugar 5g, salt 1.34g

Indian-spiced shepherd's pie

Give an old favourite a new twist with this spicy version – top with diced potatoes sprinkled with the superspice turmeric. The whole family will love this.

 1 hour 5 minutes   6

- 500g pack lean minced lamb
- 1 onion, chopped
- 2 carrots, diced
- 2 tbsp garam masala
- 200ml/7fl oz hot stock (lamb, beef or chicken)
- 200g/7oz frozen peas
- 800g/1lb 12oz potatoes, diced
- 1 tsp ground turmeric
- small bunch coriander leaves, roughly chopped
- juice ½ lemon, plus wedges to garnish

1 Heat oven to 200C/180C fan/gas 6. In a non-stick frying pan, cook the lamb, onion and carrots, stirring often, until the lamb is browned and the vegetables are starting to soften, about 8 minutes. Add the garam masala and some seasoning, and cook for a further 2 minutes. Pour in the stock, bring to the boil, tip in the peas and cook for a further 2 minutes until most of the liquid has evaporated.

2 Meanwhile, cook the potatoes in a large pan of salted boiling water until just tender, about 8 minutes. Drain well, return to the pan and gently stir in the turmeric and coriander – try not to break up the potatoes too much.

3 Transfer the mince mixture to a baking dish and top with the turmeric potatoes. Squeeze over the lemon juice, then bake for 30–35 minutes until the potatoes are golden. Serve immediately with extra lemon wedges on the side, if you like.

PER SERVING 317 kcals, protein 22g, carbs 32g, fat 12g, sat fat 5g, fibre 4g, sugar 5g, salt 0.44g

Porcini-rubbed steak

· ·

Dried porcini mushrooms make this treat for two a must-try for steak lovers – adding dried mushrooms is a great way of enriching the flavour and packs in extra nutrients.

🕐 10 minutes, plus marinating 🄯 2

- 25g/1oz dried porcini mushrooms
- 1 thyme sprig, leaves only
- 2 thick beef sirloin steaks
- 1 tbsp olive oil
- baked potatoes and green salad, to serve

1 Whizz the mushrooms into a fine powder in a small food processor or coffee grinder. Mix with a good pinch of salt, some black pepper and the thyme leaves. Rub the mixture all over the steaks, then pop them on to a plate or into a sealable kitchen bag and chill overnight to marinate.

2 Brush away any excess mixture from the steaks. Heat a griddle pan until smoking hot, turn the heat to medium, then smear the olive oil over one side of each steak. Griddle, oiled-side down, for 3 minutes. Turn over (there's no need to oil the other side), then cook for another 2 minutes for medium–rare, 4 minutes for well-done. Serve with a baked potato and salad.

· ·
PER SERVING 428 kcals, protein 47g, carbs 1g, fat 26g, sat fat 10g, fibre 2g, sugar none, salt 0.29g

Asian short ribs with herb salad

. . . .

A Thai-style beef recipe that's made in a pressure cooker – the meat becomes melt-in-the-mouth in its rich, delicious sauce. Serve simply with cooked basmati rice.

 1 hour 20 minutes   4

- large piece ginger, finely chopped
- large pack coriander, stalks and leaves separated
- 1 red onion, finely chopped
- 3 garlic cloves, crushed
- 1 tbsp vegetable oil
- 4 beef short ribs
- 1 tsp golden caster sugar
- 1 tbsp dark soy sauce
- 3 star anise
- 50ml/2fl oz oyster sauce
- 500ml/18fl oz chicken stock
- 2 tbsp Chinese black rice wine vinegar
- cooked basmati rice, to serve

FOR THE HERB SALAD
- 1 Thai red chilli, chopped
- small pack mint leaves
- 1 shallot, finely sliced
- juice 1 lime
- 1 tsp Thai fish sauce

1 In a mini chopper, make a paste with the ginger, coriander stalks, onion and garlic, then set aside.

2 Heat the oil in the pressure-cooker pan and brown the meat well on all sides, then remove to a plate. Fry the paste for 2–3 minutes with the sugar. Return the ribs to the pan and add the soy sauce, star anise, oyster sauce and enough of the stock to just cover the ribs.

3 Bring to a simmer, cover and bring up to high pressure. Cook for 45 minutes, then release the pressure slowly. Take off the lid, add the vinegar and remove the ribs from the pan. Simmer the sauce down until reduced and intensely flavoured.

4 While the sauce is simmering, mix the salad ingredients together with the coriander leaves. Serve each rib in a puddle of sauce, topped with a pile of salad and some cooked basmati rice on the side.

. . . .

PER SERVING 504 kcals, protein 26g, carbs 9g, fat 40g, sat fat 16g, fibre 2g, sugar 5g, salt 2.9g

Papaya with lime & blueberries

A healthy dessert that makes the most of just three ingredients, plus you'll be contributing to your 5-a-day. Select ripe papaya to enhance the natural sweetness.

 5 minutes 4

- 2 ripe papayas
- 2 limes
- 2 handfuls blueberries

1 Halve the papayas lengthways. Scoop out and discard the seeds, and sit the papaya halves on four serving plates.
2 Squeeze the juice from 1½ of the limes. Cut the remaining ½ lime into four wedges.
3 Pour the lime juice over the papaya halves, scatter the blueberries over and serve with the lime wedges.

PER SERVING 59 kcals, protein 1g, carbs 14g, fat none, sat fat none, fibre 3g, sugar 9g, salt 0.02g

Grapefruit, orange & apricot salad

A couple of dollops of natural yogurt will finish off this fruity salad nicely.

 10 minutes   4

- 2 grapefruits
- 2 oranges
- 4 apricots, stoned and sliced
- natural yogurt, to serve

1 First segment the grapefruits and oranges. One by one, cut a little horizontal slice from the top and bottom of each fruit so that they can sit flat on a board. Using a small, sharp knife, cut off the peel and pith in downward strokes, following the curve of the fruit. Work your way round until all the peel is removed.

2 Hold the fruit over a bowl to catch the juice and then cut free each segment by carefully slicing between the membranes to release it. Put the segments into the bowl of juice and gently stir in the apricot slices. Serve with a generous dollop of natural yogurt, if you like.

PER SERVING 67 kcals, protein 2g, carbs 13g, fat none, sat fat none, fibre 4g, sugar 13g, salt none.

Instant frozen-berry yogurt

Craving something sweet after dinner? Keep a bag of mixed berries in your freezer, yogurt in the fridge, and this easy pudding is just minutes away.

 2 minutes  4

- 250g/9oz frozen berries, plus extra for serving (optional)
- 250g/9oz fat-free Greek yogurt
- 1 tbsp agave syrup, honey or maple syrup (to taste)

1 Blend the frozen berries, Greek yogurt and agave syrup, honey or maple syrup in a food processor for 20 seconds, until they form a smooth ice-cream texture.
2 Scoop into four bowls and scatter with extra whole berries to serve, if you like.

PER SERVING 70 kcals, protein 7g, carbs 9g, fat none, sat fat none, fibre 2g, sugar 9g, salt 0.1g

Pink grapefruit, raspberry & mint jellies

A refreshing change from sugary packaged jellies, these make a light, elegant finish to a meal.

🕐 20 minutes, plus chilling   🥧 6

- 5 sheets of leaf gelatine
- 15g/½oz mint leaves, roughly chopped
- 1 pink grapefruit
- 100g/4oz small raspberries
- 2 ripe peaches, peeled, stoned and chopped

1 Soak the gelatine in a bowl of cold water. Boil 1 litre/1¾ pints water in the kettle and pour it over the mint leaves. Leave the mint to infuse for 5 minutes then strain the liquid into a large jug. Squeeze the excess moisture from the soaked gelatine then stir the gelatine into the hot mint mixture until dissolved. Set aside to cool.

2 Cut the peel and pith from the grapefruit with a sharp knife then cut between the segments to release them, reserving any juice. Cut the segments into about three pieces each then distribute the grapefruit, raspberries and peaches among six glasses. Stir the reserved grapefruit juice into the cooled mint jelly then pour the jelly into the glasses and chill until set.

PER JELLY 38 kcals, protein 2g, carbs 6g, fat none, sat fat none, fibre 2g, sugar 3g, salt none

Blueberry & lemon pancakes

To lift this breakfast sweet to a dessert, add a scoop of crème fraîche and some extra berries, or for brunch dollop on some natural yogurt and a drizzle of maple syrup.

 30 minutes 14

- 200g/7oz plain flour
- 1 tsp cream of tartar
- ½ tsp bicarbonate of soda
- 1 tsp maple syrup
- 75g/2½oz blueberries
- zest 1 lemon
- 200ml/7fl oz milk
- 1 egg
- knob butter, for cooking

1 Put the flour, cream of tartar and bicarbonate of soda in a bowl, and mix well with a fork. Drop the maple syrup into the dry ingredients along with the blueberries and lemon zest.

2 Pour the milk into a measuring jug and beat in the egg. Add most of the milk mixture to the flour mix and mix well. Keep adding more of the milk mix until you get a smooth, thick pouring batter.

3 Heat a frying pan and brush the base with a little of the butter. Then spoon in the batter, a tablespoon at a time, in heaps. Bubbles will appear on top as the pancakes cook – turn them at this stage. Cook until brown on the second side, then keep warm on a plate, covered with foil. Repeat until all the mixture is used up.

PER PANCAKE 73 kcals, protein 2g, carbs 12g, fat 1g, sat fat 1g, fibre 1g, sugar 2g, salt 0.1g

Coconut crêpes with raspberry sauce

We've elevated the humble pancake to a smart, sophisticated pudding. Our sweetener for the raspberry sauce is maple syrup, which is rich in minerals like zinc and calcium.

 45 minutes 6

FOR THE RASPBERRY SAUCE
- 200g/7oz raspberries, plus 6 extra
- 2 tsp cornflour
- 2 tsp maple syrup

FOR THE COCONUT CRÊPES
- 140g/5oz plain flour
- 2 eggs
- 300ml/½ pint coconut milk
- 2 tbsp toasted desiccated coconut
- a little sunflower oil, for frying

1 Quarter the 6 raspberries. Mix the cornflour with 1 tablespoon water until smooth, stir into 300ml/½ pint water and heat, stirring until thickened. Add the remaining raspberries and cook gently, mashing the berries to a pulp. Rub the mixture through a sieve into a bowl to remove the seeds. Stir in the quartered berries and the maple syrup.

2 For the crêpes, tip the flour and a pinch of salt into a jug then beat in the eggs, coconut milk, 200ml/7fl oz water and 1½ tablespoons of the toasted coconut until the consistency of double cream. Thin with water if necessary.

3 Heat a small frying pan with a dash of oil then pour in a little batter, swirling it so it covers the base of the pan. Leave over the heat for a minute until brown underneath, then carefully flip it over and cook the other side for a few seconds more. Transfer to a plate and repeat with the remaining batter. Stir the batter to redistribute the coconut as you use it.

4 Serve two crêpes per person, drizzled with sauce and scattered with toasted coconut.

PER SERVING 265 kcals, protein 6g, carbs 24g, fat 15g, sat fat 11g, fibre 3g, sugar 4g, salt 0.2g

Mascarpone & pineapple cheesecake

Canned pineapple is used to sweeten this gelatine-set cheesecake. Leaf gelatine is easier to use than powdered, just soak it in cold water then dissolve in warm liquid.

 40 minutes, plus chilling 12

FOR THE BASE
- 40g/1½oz butter
- 100g/4oz oatcakes, crushed to crumbs
- 25g/1oz toasted desiccated coconut
- oil, for greasing

FOR THE TOPPING
- 425g can pineapple in natural juice, drained
- 5 sheets of leaf gelatine
- 250g tub reduced-fat mascarpone
- 500g tub full-fat fromage frais
- 160g can coconut cream
- grated zest ½ lemon

1 Melt the butter for the base in a pan and stir in the biscuit crumbs and all but 1 tablespoon of the coconut. Mix well then press very firmly on to the base of a lightly oiled 21cm-round springform cake tin to make a firm layer. Chill.

2 Finely chop a slice of pineapple for the topping then pulse the remainder to a pulp in a food processor or with a hand blender. Soak the gelatine in cold water to soften it. In a bowl beat together the mascarpone and fromage frais.

3 Very gently warm the coconut cream in a small pan. Squeeze the excess moisture from the gelatine, add the gelatine to the warm coconut and stir until melted. Stir into the mascarpone mixture with the crushed and chopped pineapple and lemon zest then pour on to the biscuit base and chill until set.

4 Carefully remove the cheesecake from the tin, slide onto a plate and decorate with the reserved coconut around the edge.

PER SERVING 213 kcals, protein 6g, carbs 10g, fat 16g, sat fat 10g, fibre 1g, sugar 5g, salt 0.2g

Baked banana cheesecake

We promise you won't miss the sugar in this ingenious sugar-free cheesecake. Serve it to friends and family and see if they guess what's missing!

 1 hour, plus cooling and chilling   12

FOR THE BASE
- oil, for greasing
- 50g/2oz butter
- 75g/2½oz oatcakes, finely crushed
- 50g/2oz cream crackers
- 1 tbsp cocoa powder, plus extra for dusting
- 15g/1oz salted peanuts, very finely chopped

FOR THE TOPPING
- 2 small ripe bananas
- juice 1 lemon
- 2 x 250g tubs ricotta
- 200g tub Greek yogurt
- 4 eggs
- ½ tsp sugar-free vanilla extract
- 2 tbsp cornflour
- 100ml/3½fl oz double cream

1 Heat oven to 180C/160C fan/gas 4 and lightly oil a non-stick loose-based 22cm-round cake tin. Melt the butter for the base in a pan and stir in both the biscuits, the cocoa and the peanuts until well coated. Press on to the base of the tin to make a firm layer and bake for 10 minutes. Remove from the oven and increase the oven to 240C/220C fan/gas 9.

2 To make the filling, mash the bananas with the lemon juice in a large bowl then beat in the ricotta, yogurt, eggs, vanilla and cornflour until everything is very well mixed. Pour on to the biscuit base and bake for 10 minutes, then lower the oven to 110C/90C fan/gas ¼ and cook for 25 minutes more. Turn off the oven and leave the cheesecake inside to cool. When cold, chill. Cooking the cheesecake this way should prevent it from cracking.

3 To serve, remove the cheesecake from the tin and slide on to a plate. Beat the cream until it just holds its shape then smooth over the top of the cheesecake and lightly dust with cocoa.

PER SERVING 258 kcals, protein 9g, carbs 13g, fat 18g, sat fat 10g, fibre 1g, sugar 4g, salt 0.4g

Baked lemon & vanilla rice pudding

Always a family favourite, the uplifting zing of lemon zest cuts through the richness of this comforting classic. Perfect for a Sunday-lunch pud.

🕐 1 hour 40 minutes, plus resting   4-6

- 600ml/1 pint milk
- 500ml/16fl oz single cream
- zest 1 lemon
- 1 vanilla pod, split
- 25g/1oz caster sugar
- 100g/4oz pudding rice
- 25g/1oz butter, diced, plus extra for greasing

1 Heat oven to 140C/120C fan/gas 1. Put the milk, cream, lemon zest and vanilla pod in a pan. Gently bring to a simmer, then stir in the caster sugar and rice.

2 Pour the mixture into a greased shallow ovenproof dish and dot the butter on top. Bake for 30 minutes, then stir well and cook for 1 hour more until the pudding is soft and creamy and a golden skin has formed on top. The depth and type of dish you use will affect the cooking time, so if the pudding seems too loose, return it to the oven and check every 10 minutes or so. Once cooked, leave the pudding to rest for 10 minutes before serving.

PER SERVING (6) 340 kcals, protein 7g, carbs 24g, fat 24g, sat fat 15g, fibre none, sugar 10g, salt 0.2g

Cinnamon apple-pecan pudding

. . . .

We've used xylitol to sweeten our scrumptious apple pudding. Xylitol is a naturally occurring carbohydrate that looks like table sugar but has just a third of the calories.

 55 minutes    6

- 85g/3oz softened butter
- 85g/3oz xylitol
- 125g/4½oz self-raising flour
- 25g/1oz rolled oats
- 1 tsp ground cinnamon
- 1 heaped tsp baking powder
- 2 eggs
- 3 tbsp milk
- 1 Bramley apple (about 250g/9oz), peeled, cored and diced into small chunks
- 25g/1oz pecan nuts, roughly chopped or broken

1 Heat oven to 180C/160C fan/gas 4 and lightly grease a 1-litre (20 x 16cm) pie or oven dish. Tip the butter and xylitol into a bowl with the flour, oats, cinnamon and baking powder. Break in the eggs, add the milk, then beat with an electric hand whisk until evenly mixed and smooth. Stir in the apple, then scrape into the dish, level the top and scatter with the pecans.

2 Bake for 35–45 minutes until risen and golden and a skewer inserted into the centre comes out clean. Serve with Greek yogurt or cream, if you like.

. . . .

PER SERVING 328 kcals, protein 6g, carbs 36g, fat 17g, sat fat 8g, fibre 3g, sugar 5g, salt 0.8g

Custard & nutmeg tart

Dried fruits are super sweet. In this tart sultanas act as natural sweeteners, but you could use dates, prunes or raisins to reduce the amount of added sugar.

⏱ 1 hour 20 minutes, includes chilling   🍽 10

- 500ml/18fl oz whole milk
- 4 eggs
- 25g/1oz sultanas
- 1 tsp sugar-free vanilla extract
- nutmeg, for grating
- finely grated zest 1 orange
- 250g/9oz ready-made shortcrust pastry
- plain flour, for dusting

1 Beat the milk and eggs together, strain into a jug and stir in the sultanas, vanilla, a generous grating of nutmeg and the orange zest. Set aside to allow the flavours to mingle.

2 Heat oven to 200C/180C fan/gas 6 with a baking sheet inside. Thinly roll out the pastry on a lightly floured surface until large enough to line a loose-bottomed 23cm-round tart tin, leaving the excess pastry overhanging at the top. Chill for 20 minutes. Line the pastry case with baking paper, fill with baking beans and cook on the heated sheet for 15 minutes. Remove the beans and paper, and bake for 5 minutes more to cook the base of the tart. Turn the heat down to 180C/160C fan/gas 4. Trim round the edge of the pastry case with a sharp knife to remove the excess.

3 Very carefully pour the custard mixture into the tart case, evenly distributing the sultanas then grate over some more nutmeg. Bake for 30 minutes until the custard is set but still has a wobble in the centre. Cool to room temperature or chill before serving.

PER SERVING 187 kcals, protein 6g, carbs 15g, fat 11g, sat fat 4g, fibre 1g, sugar 4g, salt 0.4g

Sugar-free lemon-drizzle cake

Sweetened with all-natural xylitol, this sponge has a dense, syrupy texture and keeps well for a few days.

 1 hour 20 minutes 8–10 slices

- 225g/8oz self-raising flour, sifted
- ½ tsp baking powder
- 225g/8oz xylitol
- zest 2 lemons
- 2 eggs, at room temperature
- 125ml/4fl oz sunflower oil
- 1 tbsp milk
- 200g/7oz 0%-fat Greek yogurt

FOR THE DRIZZLE
- juice 1 lemon
- 50g/2oz xylitol

1 Heat oven to 180C/160C fan/gas 4. Grease and line a 1.2-litre loaf tin with baking parchment. Mix together the flour, baking powder, xylitol and lemon zest in a large bowl.

2 Mix the eggs, sunflower oil, milk and yogurt together in a separate bowl or jug, and stir the wet mix into the flour mixture.

3 Spoon the cake mix into a tin and smooth the surface. Transfer to the oven immediately, bake on the middle shelf for 1 hour–1 hour 10 minutes. Check after 50 minutes – if the cake is becoming too dark, cover loosely with foil.

4 Just before the end of cooking time, make the drizzle by heating the lemon juice and xylitol in a small bowl. Stir over a low heat until the xylitol has dissolved. Once the cake is cooked, take it out of the oven and pour over the drizzle.

5 Cool in the tin before turning it out and slicing to serve.

PER SLICE (10) 323 kcals, protein 5g, carbs 44g, fat 14g, sat fat 2g, fibre 1g, sugar 1g, salt 0.3g

Sugar-free carrot cake

This dairy-free, sugar-free carrot cake uses xylitol to sweeten it – simple to make and delicious.

🕐 1 hour 25 minutes   🥧 6–8 slices

- butter, for greasing
- 100g/4oz pecan nuts
- 140g/5oz self-raising flour, sieved
- 2 tsp ground cinnamon
- 1 tsp bicarbonate of soda
- 140g/5oz xylitol
- 2 eggs (at room temperature)
- 140ml/4½fl oz rapeseed oil
- 175g/6oz grated carrots
- 100g/4oz sultanas
- natural yogurt, to serve

1 Heat oven to 180C/160C fan/gas 4. Grease and line an 18cm round cake tin with baking parchment. Set aside 12 of the pecans and roughly chop the rest.

2 In a large bowl, mix together the flour, cinnamon, bicarbonate of soda, xylitol and chopped pecans.

3 In a separate bowl or jug, beat the eggs and rapeseed oil together. Pour into the flour mixture and stir until combined. Stir through the carrots and sultanas. Spoon into the lined tin, smooth the surface and press whole pecans to form a circle around the edge.

4 Cook for 1 hour–1 hour 10 minutes until the top feels springy to the touch and a skewer inserted into the cake comes out clean. Check after 50 minutes, if the cake is becoming too dark, cover loosely with foil. Cool on a wire rack for 10 minutes, then turn out and allow to cool. Serve slightly warm or cold. This cake keeps for up to 5 days in a tin. Serve with a dollop of natural yogurt.

PER SLICE (8) 438 kcals, protein 5g, carbs 40g, fat 28g, sat fat 2g, fibre 3g, sugar 10g, salt 0.5g

Moroccan orange & cardamom cake

Puréeing the whole boiled oranges means we don't need oil or butter. You can cook them in the microwave; pierce them through then cook on High for 6 minutes.

 2½ hours   10–12

- 2 oranges, scrubbed
- 6 green cardamoms, seeds removed and crushed
- 225g pack xylitol
- 6 eggs
- 200g pack ground almonds
- 50g/2oz polenta
- 25g/1oz self-raising flour
- 2 tsp baking powder
- 15g/½oz flaked almonds
- 0%-fat Greek yogurt, to serve

1 Put the whole oranges in a pan and cover with water, then boil, covered, for 1 hour until a knife easily pierces them. If the oranges won't stay under the water put a small pan lid on top. Remove the oranges from the water and cool, then quarter and remove any seeds and pith. Blitz the flesh to a rough purée with a hand blender or food processor and put in a large bowl.

2 Heat oven to 160C/140C fan/gas 3 and line the base and sides of a 21cm-round loose-bottomed cake tin with baking paper. Beat the cardamom, xylitol and eggs into the orange purée, then mix the ground almonds with the polenta, flour and baking powder and fold in until well blended.

3 Scrape the mixture into the tin, level the top and bake for 40 minutes. Scatter over the almonds, return to the oven and bake for 20–25 minutes more until a skewer inserted into the centre comes out clean. Remove from the tin and leave to cool. Serve as a cake or as a dessert with Greek yogurt.

PER SLICE (12) 257 kcals, protein 8g, carbs 26g, fat 13g, sat fat 2g, fibre 1g, sugar 2g, salt 0.3g

Strawberry & white-chocolate choux buns

Thought a low-sugar diet meant no treats? Think again! These delicious choux buns make a great dinner-party finale.

 1 hour 10 minutes   8

FOR THE CHOUX PASTRY
- 50g/2oz butter
- 75g/2½oz plain flour
- 2 eggs, beaten with 1 tbsp water
- 1 tbsp flaked almonds (optional)

FOR THE FILLING
- 2 tbsp custard powder
- 300ml/½ pint semi-skimmed milk
- ½ tsp sugar-free vanilla extract
- 150ml/¼ pint Greek yogurt
- 15g/½oz coarsely grated chocolate

TO DECORATE
- 125g/4½oz small strawberries, halved
- ⅛ tsp icing sugar (optional)

1 Line a large baking sheet with baking paper. Heat oven to 200C/180C fan/gas 6. Melt the butter in a non-stick pan with 125ml/4fl oz water. Bring to a boil, remove from the heat and beat in the flour until the mixture comes together as a ball. Cool for 5 minutes then beat in the eggs to make a thick glossy mix.

2 Spoon on to the baking sheet in eight blobs then poke in the almonds, if using. Bake for 25–30 minutes until well risen and golden. Slash the sides and cook for 5 minutes to dry.

3 Mix the custard powder with a little milk, then add to the remaining milk and vanilla in a pan and cook, stirring, until thickened. Cool for 5 minutes, beat in the yogurt and set aside, stirring to prevent a skin forming. When cold, stir in the grated chocolate.

4 Reserve 1 tablespoon of custard and fill the buns with the rest and with the strawberries, keeping 4 halves for the tops. Stick on with the custard. Dust with icing sugar, if using.

. . . .
PER BUN 177 kcals, protein 5g, carbs 15g, fat 12g, sat fat 6g, fibre 1g, sugar 4g, salt 0.3g

Nutty blueberry muffins

These great-tasting buttermilk muffins are delicious served warm from the oven.

 35 minutes 12

- 1-cal oil spray, for greasing
- 200g/7oz self-raising flour
- 100g/4oz hazelnuts, with or without skin, lightly toasted
- ½ tsp bicarbonate of soda
- 284ml pot buttermilk
- 100ml/3½fl oz skimmed milk
- 3 eggs
- 2 tbsp agave syrup
- 75ml/2½fl oz rapeseed oil (we used butter flavoured)
- 100g/4oz blueberries

1 Heat oven to 180C/160C fan/gas 4. Lightly grease a 12-hole silicone muffin tin with oil spray, or line with paper cases. Put the flour and hazelnuts in a food processor and whizz until the nuts are finely ground. Tip into a bowl and stir in the bicarbonate of soda. Whisk together the buttermilk, milk, eggs, agave and oil.

2 Mix the wet ingredients into the dry until smooth, taking care not to overwork the mix, then stir in the blueberries. Divide the mixture among the muffin holes or cases and bake for 20 minutes until a skewer poked in the centre comes out clean. Leave to cool for 10 minutes, before turning out of the tin. If freezing, defrost at room temperature, then warm through in the oven.

PER MUFFIN 211 kcals, protein 5g, carbs 18g, fat 13g, sat fat 1g, fibre 2g, sugar 5g, salt 0.4g

Welsh rarebit muffins

These muffins are yummy served warm, but they also keep well for a few days, making them ideal for lunchboxes.

 40 minutes 12

- 225g/8oz self-raising flour
- 50g/2oz plain flour
- 1 tsp baking powder
- ½ level tsp bicarbonate of soda
- ¼ tsp salt
- ½ level tsp English mustard powder
- 100g/4oz strong cheese, half grated, half cubed
- 6 tbsp vegetable oil
- 150g/5½oz Greek yogurt
- 125ml/4fl oz milk
- 1 egg
- 1 tbsp Worcestershire sauce

1 Heat oven to 200C/180C fan/gas 6 and line a 12-hole muffin tin with 12 muffin cases. Mix together the self-raising and plain flours, baking powder, bicarbonate of soda, salt and mustard powder in a bowl.
2 In a separate bowl, mix the cheese, oil, yogurt, milk, egg and Worcestershire sauce.
3 Combine all the ingredients, taking care not to overmix, and divide the mixture among the muffin cases. Bake in the oven for 20–25 minutes or until golden. Remove and cool slightly on a wire rack.

PER MUFFIN 189 kcals, protein 6g, carbs 19g, fat 11g, sat fat 4g, fibre 1g, sugar 1g, salt 0.79g

Cheddar-sage scones

Make sure you use a punchy, mature cheese for these savoury scones.

 25 minutes   8

- 225g/8oz self-raising flour
- 1½ tsp English mustard powder
- 50g/2oz cold butter, cubed
- 100g/4oz mature Cheddar, grated
- 1 tbsp finely chopped sage leaves, plus 8 small leaves
- 1 egg, beaten
- 100ml/3½fl oz buttermilk

1 Heat oven to 220C/200C fan/gas 7. Mix the flour, mustard powder, ½ teaspoon salt and a grinding of black pepper in a large bowl. Rub in the butter until the mixture resembles fine crumbs. Stir in half of the cheese and the sage. Mix together the egg and buttermilk in a separate bowl.

2 Make a well in the centre of the flour mix and pour in all but ½ tablespoon of the buttermilk mix. Working quickly, stir until the mixture forms a soft, spongy dough. Tip on to a lightly floured surface and knead briefly until smooth. Roll out to a 3cm/1¼in-thick square. Cut into quarters, then half each quarter diagonally, so you have eight triangles.

3 Put the scones on a floured baking sheet, brush with the remaining egg–buttermilk mix, sprinkle over the remaining cheese and top each with a sage leaf. Bake for 12–14 minutes until they are well risen, golden and sound hollow when tapped on the bottom. Eat while still warm, spread with butter.

PER SCONE 207 kcals, protein 7g, carbs 21g, fat 11g, sat fat 6g, fibre 1g, sugar 1g, salt 0.6g

Cheddar & bacon buns

You'll love these savoury buns for breakfast, brunch or your lunchbox. The secret to light buns is to stop mixing before you think you should.

 40 minutes  6 large buns

- 1 tsp oil, plus extra for greasing
- 4 rashers streaky bacon, cut into small pieces
- 50g/2oz mature Cheddar
- 175g/6oz plain flour
- 1 tsp baking powder
- 1 tsp English mustard
- 2 eggs
- 85g/3oz butter, melted
- 200ml/7fl oz milk
- 1 tbsp parsley leaves, chopped

1 Heat oven to 180C/160C fan/gas 4 and grease six wells of a muffin tin with a little oil.
2 Heat the oil in a frying pan and fry the bacon until crisp. Tip out on to kitchen paper and allow to cool. Cut two-thirds of the cheese into little pieces and finely grate the rest.
3 Sift the flour, baking powder, ½ teaspoon of salt and a little black pepper into a bowl. Whisk the mustard, eggs, butter and milk in a jug. Pour the wet mix into the dry and stir a few times until just combined. Add the bacon, cheese pieces and parsley, being careful not to overwork the mix.
4 Spoon the bun mix into the greased wells (they will be quite full), sprinkle each with a little grated cheese, then bake for 25 minutes or until golden, risen and firm to the touch.

PER BUN 322 kcals, protein 12g, carbs 25g, fat 20g, sat fat 11g, fibre 1g, sugar 2g, salt 1.63g

Cheese wheatmeal biscuits

Savoury, oaty biscuits that are great for lunchboxes. Add Marmite or peanut butter for a delicious pinwheel.

 35 minutes 20–30 biscuits, depending on cutter size

- 100g/4oz wholemeal flour
- 50g/2oz self-raising flour
- 25g/1oz medium oatmeal
- 100g/4oz butter
- 100g/4oz Cheddar, finely grated
- 1 egg yolk

1 Heat oven to 180C/160C fan/gas 4. Put the flours and oatmeal into a bowl and rub in the butter. Stir in the cheese. Add the egg yolk and mix in using a fork. When the mixture starts to clump together, use your hands to knead to a smooth dough.

2 Put the dough between two sheets of baking parchment and roll out thinly to about 0.5cm/½in. Cut out the desired shapes and lift them using a palette knife on to a non-stick baking sheet. Reroll any trimmings and cut out more shapes, or take walnut-sized pieces of dough, roll into balls and put on the baking tray, flattening them slightly with a fork.

3 Bake in the oven for 12–14 minutes until golden brown. Leave on the baking sheet for a few minutes to firm up before removing to a wire cooling rack.

PER BISCUIT (20) 90 kcals, protein 2g, carbs 6g, fat 6g, sat fat 4g, fibre 0.8g, sugar trace, salt 0.2g

Malted nut & seed loaf

Add seeds, nuts and wholemeal flour to a basic dough for a bread with bags of flavour and nutrients. It stays fresh in an airtight container for 3 days, or freeze it for 1 month.

🕐 1 hour, plus rising   🍰 Cuts into 12 slices

- 500g/1lb 2oz strong wholemeal flour, plus extra for rolling
- 7g sachet fast-action yeast
- 100g/4oz mixed seeds (we used a mix of linseed, hemp seeds, pumpkin seeds and sesame seeds)
- 50g/2oz walnut pieces
- up to 350ml/12fl oz lukewarm water
- a little sunflower oil, for greasing

1 Mix the flour and yeast plus 1 tablespoon salt together in a large bowl and make a well in the middle. Stir in the seeds, reserving 1 tablespoon, and the nuts. Pour in the water and mix to a slightly wet dough. Tip out on to a lightly floured surface and knead for 10 minutes or until smooth and elastic. Put in a clean, oiled bowl, cover and leave to rise in a warm place until doubled in size. Roll the dough around in the reserved seeds, then lift the bread on to a baking sheet to prove for about 30 minutes until doubled in size.

2 Heat oven to 220C/200C fan/gas 7. Bake the bread for 15 minutes, then lower the oven temperature to 190C/170C fan/gas 5 and continue to bake for 30 minutes until the loaf sounds hollow when removed from the tin and tapped on the base. Leave on a wire rack to cool completely.

PER SLICE 172 kcals, protein 7g, carbs 28g, fat 4g, sat fat 1g, fibre 5g, sugar 1g, salt 0.43g

Rye bread

Rye is a fabulous grain for managing your body's response to glucose and for keeping you fuller for longer.

 50 minutes, plus rising   Cuts into 8 slices

- 200g/7oz rye flour, plus extra for dusting
- 200g/7oz strong white or wholemeal flour
- 7g sachet fast-action dried yeast
- 1 tbsp honey
- a little sunflower oil, for greasing
- 1 tsp caraway seeds (optional)

1 Tip the flours, yeast and ½ teaspoon fine salt into a bowl. In a jug, mix the honey with 250ml warm water, pour into the flour and mix to form a dough. If the dough looks too dry add more warm water. Knead for 10 minutes until smooth. Rye contains less gluten than wheat flour so the dough won't feel as springy.

2 Put the dough in a well-oiled bowl, cover with cling film and leave to rise in a warm place for 1–2 hours, or until roughly doubled in size. Dust a 900g loaf tin with flour.

3 Tip the dough on to a floured work surface and knead briefly to knock out any air bubbles. Add the caraway seeds, if using. Shape into a smooth oval loaf and pop into the tin. Cover with oiled cling film and leave to rise for 1–1½ hours, or until doubled in size.

4 Heat oven to 220C/200C fan/gas 7. Remove the cling film and dust the loaf with rye flour. Slash the top then bake for 30 minutes until dark brown and hollow sounding when tapped. Transfer to a wire cooling rack and cool for at least 20 minutes.

PER SERVING (8 slices) 170 kcals, protein 6g, carbs 34g, fat 1g, sat fat 0.2g, fibre 7g, sugar 2g, salt 0.3g

Sun-dried tomato & soda bread baps

With a healthy helping of magnesium-rich oats, these craggy bread buns use bicarbonate of soda instead of yeast – serve with a scraping of butter or soft cheese.

 40 minutes    6

- 250g/9oz plain white flour, plus extra for dusting
- 250g/9oz seed and grain bread flour
- 100g/4oz porridge oats
- 1 tsp bicarbonate of soda
- 1 tsp dried thyme
- 25g/1oz butter
- 85g/3oz sun-dried tomatoes (from a jar), roughly chopped
- 475ml/16fl oz buttermilk

1 Heat oven to 200C/180C fan/gas 6 and dust a baking sheet with flour. Mix the flours, oats, bicarbonate of soda, 1 teaspoon salt and thyme in a bowl, then rub in the butter.

2 Add the tomatoes, pour in the buttermilk and mix quickly with the blade of a knife to make a wet dough. Tip on to a floured work surface, then cut evenly into six and, with floured hands, shape to make six rounds. Handle the dough as little as possible – not just because it is sticky but also to make sure the texture stays light. Arrange, spaced apart, on the baking sheet and mark a cross in the tops with a floured knife.

3 Bake for 20–25 minutes until the bases of the baps are pale golden and sound hollow when tapped. Cover with a tea towel and leave to cool. To freeze, pack the cooled baps into a rigid container. Thaw at room temperature for 3 hours.

PER BAP 492 kcals, protein 15g, carbs 74g, fat 14g, sat fat 4g, fibre 5g, sugar 5g, salt 1.8g

Indian breads with courgette & coriander

This Indian bread is called thelpa; serve with small bowls of natural yogurt.

 1 hour   12

- ½ tsp cumin seeds
- 450g/1lb courgettes, coarsely grated
- 175g/6oz plain flour, plus extra for rolling out
- 175g/6oz wholemeal flour
- 2 tsp ginger, grated
- pinch ground turmeric
- small handful coriander, leaves chopped
- 3–4 tbsp sunflower oil

1 Dry-fry the cumin seeds for 1 minute in a non-stick pan until toasted.

2 Mix the grated courgettes, flours, ginger, turmeric and coriander in a large bowl with 1 teaspoon salt. Rub in 1½ tablespoons of the oil, then slowly mix in 4–5 tablespoons cold water until a soft dough forms. Tear into 12 pieces and shape into balls.

3 Using a little extra flour, roll each piece into a thin 14cm/5½in round. Heat a griddle or heavy-based frying pan until very hot. Add one or two breads and cook for 2 minutes, patting with a clean cloth – this helps the bread cook fast. Turn the breads over and cook for about 2 minutes more.

4 Drizzle over a little of the remaining oil, turn the breads again for 30–60 seconds more, then drizzle a few more drops of the oil on this side. Remove and repeat with the rest. Serve hot or cold.

PER SERVING 145 kcals, protein 4g, carbs 20g, fat 4g, sat fat 1g, fibre 3g, sugar 1g, salt 0.4g

Index

Also available from BBC Books and Good Food

Baking

Bakes & Cakes
Chocolate Treats
Cupcakes & Small Bakes
Easy Baking Recipes
Fruity Puds
Teatime Treats
Tempting Desserts
Traybakes

Easy

30-minute suppers
Budget Dishes
Cheap Eats
Easy Student Dinners
Easy Weeknight Suppers
More One-pot Dishes
More Slow Cooker
  Favourites
One-pot dishes
Pressure Cooker Favourites

Simple Suppers
Slow Cooker Favourites
Speedy Suppers

Eat Well

14-day Healthy Eating Diet
Fasting Day Recipes
Low-Fat Feasts

Everyday

Best-ever Chicken Recipes
Best-ever Curries
Fish & Seafood Dishes
Gluten-free Recipes
Healthy Family Food
Hot & Spicy Dishes
Italian Feasts
Low-carb Cooking
Meals for Two
Mediterranean Dishes
Pasta & Noodle Dishes
Picnics & Packed Lunches

Recipes for Kids
Storecupboard Suppers
Healthy
Healthy Chicken Recipes
Healthy Eats
Low-calorie Recipes
More Low-fat Feasts
Seasonal Salads
Superhealthy Suppers
Veggie dishes

Weekend

Barbecues and Grills
Christmas Dishes
Delicious Gifts
Dinner-party Dishes
Make Ahead Meals
Slow-cooking Recipes
Soups & Sides
Sunday Lunches